THE
MIND OF JOHN KEATS

THE
MIND OF JOHN KEATS

BY

CLARENCE DEWITT THORPE

NEW YORK / RUSSELL & RUSSELL

FIRST PUBLISHED IN 1926
REISSUED, 1964, BY RUSSELL & RUSSELL
A DIVISION OF ATHENEUM PUBLISHERS, INC.
BY ARRANGEMENT WITH FRANCES J. THORPE
L. C. CATALOG CARD NO: 64-18603
PRINTED IN THE UNITED STATES OF AMERICA

To
My Wife

" I went to the Isle of Wight, thought so much about poetry so long together that I could not get to sleep at night. . . . I was too much in solitude, and consequently was obliged to be in continual burning of thought."   Letter to Leigh Hunt, May 10, 1817.

" Then I should be most enviable — with the yearning Passion I have for the beautiful, connected and made one with the ambition of my intellect."
                          Letter to George and Georgiana Keats, October, 1818.

" Keats was a philosopher first, a poet afterwards."
                          Arthur Lynch. *John Keats Memorial Volume.*

" Keats was a philosophic poet, and for that very reason he fell into no philosophic errors in his conception of poetry."
                          A. Clutton-Brock. *John Keats Memorial Volume.*

PREFACE

THIS book is the outgrowth of an attempt to analyze the poetic mind of Keats. About ten years ago, I began a study of the development of Keats as a poet, with special reference to his growth in self restraint. I had not proceeded far before I became convinced that the key to the young poet's remarkable advance in power during the brief span of his working years could be traced largely to a natural reaction to his own serious thought on the nature of art and poetry. Accordingly, I set to work to gather together from his letters and poems all possible evidence as to what these ideas were. The total mass of this material, a few lines of poetry here, a passage from a letter there, a bit from one of his critical comments in another place, was truly astonishing. Not less revelatory was the pertinence and the import of these utterances. There began to dawn upon me a feeling that here was an aesthetic thinker of significance. And as I came to analyze and organize, this feeling ripened into a conviction.

My first objective was to discover an adequate interpretation for the famous lines from the *Ode on a Grecian Urn* which identify truth and beauty. I had often read the passage, had often heard it explained, but I must confess I had never been able to reach a satisfying conclusion. Much has been written and many things said to illuminate Keats's meaning here; however, it seems to me these lines have never been, up to this time, satisfactorily explained. And one reason is, I feel convinced, that they have never been regarded in the light of Keats's complete aesthetic theory. In my own interpretation of them, I have found it necessary to take into account all of the poet's ideas of his art, to which these lines are both the key and culmination. Consequently, my study began and ended with that significant utterance —

" 'Beauty is truth, truth beauty ' — that is all
Ye know on earth, and all ye need to know."

v

And if I have succeeded in throwing new light on these tantalizing phrases, it is entirely due to the fact that I have analyzed them as a partial statement of the startlingly comprehensive aesthetic philosophy of a young poet and genius whose thought-life, in his last years, was one long earnest search for a solution to the problems of his art.

I had finished and submitted this book before Miss Amy Lowell's new biography was released to the public, but not wishing to let my volume appear without at least a brief recognition of so important a work, I recalled my manuscript from the press in order to add a few comments to this preface and to make two or three textual revisions in places where Miss Lowell's findings were of particular relevance.

Luckily, Miss Lowell's book and mine do not overlap. Miss Lowell has contributed to Keats criticism a most admirable biography, one of the most complete and minute records, it is safe to say, of any poet's life ever made. It would seem, as commentators have already pointed out, that from the factual point of view this biography should be regarded as final and authoritative. Lovers of Keats must be ever grateful to Miss Lowell for the patient, systematic care with which she has searched out the smallest details of the poet's life, and for the loving sympathy and breadth of understanding with which she has interpreted the facts as she has found them. Miss Lowell has revealed to the world anew the manly man and the divinely gifted singer, the artist to the core, that John Keats was; she has rescued the name of Fanny Brawne from the undeserved obloquy that was settling too permanently about it; and she has done a genuine service to literature by setting a fascinated world to reading the life history of one of its greatest and truest poets.

Moreover, Miss Lowell has included in her notable book a large amount of critical material based on Keats's poems. Although of less importance than the biography proper, it is fresh, vigorous, stimulating criticism that Miss Lowell gives us, of a type that is certain to draw renewed attention to, and arouse new interest in, Keats's poetical works. That alone would make this a memorable book.

But the thought-life of Keats, Miss Lowell, like so many other critics before her, has touched upon only incidentally. Not that she lacks interest in Keats's mind; on the contrary, she is thoroughly interested: she has included in her pages some of the most striking evidence as to his thinking, and has often supplied pertinent critical comment on this evidence, but she has not in any consistent way attempted to gather together, and organize, and interpret the hundreds of bits of available material that have direct bearing on Keats's aesthetic and philosophic thought. For instance, she has made no serious effort to explain Keats's idea of beauty, passing by even the famous " Beauty is truth" lines without special analysis. Likewise, though she quotes many passages that have bearing on Keats's views of the imagination, she does not analyze and set forth what his theories were. And, again, when such vital letters as that on the Vale of Soul-Making are cited, she usually lets the extracts stand by themselves without showing their relation to the main current of Keats's thought.

That Miss Lowell fails to treat Keats's aesthetic and philosophic theory systematically is not in the least to the discredit of her work. On the contrary, to have done otherwise would have been inconsistent with the larger plan of her great book. My only point is, that a thorough examination of Miss Lowell's biography has convinced me that, in spite of its wide scope and its thoroughness in particular fields, there is still a distinct place for such a volume as mine, with its emphasis exclusively on the thought-life of Keats. The sum total of Miss Lowell's new material does not in the least tend to invalidate my findings, but rather offers confirmation and corroboration. It is therefore with renewed confidence that I offer this book to the public as a study of the poetic mind of John Keats.

ANN ARBOR, MICHIGAN,
    April, 1925.

CONTENTS

THE MIND OF JOHN KEATS

CHAPTER I

KEATS, THINKER

I

KEATS the philosophic poet is being discovered. Keats the lover of sensuous beauty, the literary artist who knew how to charm the English language into magic combinations of lovely verse, the world well knows, but Keats the thinker and philosopher is to many still an undiscovered soul. It was Stevenson who said, " Man does not live by bread alone, but by catchwords." The truth of this is well demonstrated in the traditional attitude toward Keats, who happened to leave behind him, not all explained, a few striking phrases and sentences that early became catchwords by which his readers interpreted his verse and pigeon-holed him as a poet and a man. His oft-quoted " Beauty is truth, truth beauty," and his declaration that

> A thing of beauty is a joy forever.

appeared self-explanatory. While such exclamations as " O for a life of Sensations rather than of Thoughts! " and

> Do not all charms fly
> At the mere touch of cold philosophy!

seemed even more convincing. From such passages as these it was taken for granted that Keats delighted in the sensuous to the exclusion of interest in thought and life, and they became touchstones for the interpretation of all his poetry and his character as a man.

In spite of much early and continued admiration of his poetry, there grew up in the last century a sort of legend to the effect that Keats was little better than a mere dreamer, a maker of beautiful verses who spent his days in rapt intoxication with the sensuous world. This conception was fostered by such influences as that caustic characterization of Carlyle's in his *Essay on Burns,*

> Poetry except in such cases as that of Keats, where the whole consists in a weak-eyed maudlin sensibility and a certain vague random tunefulness of nature is no separate faculty. . . . The feelings, the gifts, that exist in the poet are those that exist with more or less development in every human soul.

Carlyle was not a great literary critic, but his voice extended far. Even Matthew Arnold helped maintain the tradition by his emphasis, in an otherwise appreciative essay, on the Keats love letter:

> It is the sort of love letter of a surgeon's apprentice which one might hear read out in a breach of promise case, or in the Divorce Court. The sensuous man speaks in it, and the sensuous man of a badly bred and badly trained sort.

Such popular critics as George William Dawson have probably done even more to keep the ghost astir. In Mr. Dawson's *Makers of Modern Poetry,* we find such sentences as this:

> Byron and Shelley were both filled with the fervor of the revolutionary spirit; but in Keats there is no trace of either. He had no interest in man. In the passion and struggle of ordinary human life, he discovered no food for poetry. . . . The only thought he has elaborated in all his writings is that beauty is worthy of worship, and loveliness should be worshipped for its own sake. The worship of loveliness he thus substituted for the worship of truth, and this seems to have satisfied all the religious instincts of his nature.

Now, whether we like to admit it or not, it is this sort of thing that the rank and file of people who know anything at all about Keats believe. It is what high school youngsters learn about him in their literature classes. It is in the air. It slips into our histories; it is the impression that gets abroad. In M. Jusserand's abridged history of English literature, in the page and a half devoted to Keats, one finds this paragraph:

Le démon Philosophique agitat l'âme de Shelley et la troublait au point de la remplir de ténèbres et de tempêtes; jusque dans les vers d'amour de Shelley paraît sa passion pour la réforme du monde. De ces rêves et de ces aspirations Keats ne se soucie nullement, réformer n'est point son affaire; admirer, désirer, aimer, voilà ce qui occupe son âme et sa coeur. Il admire, il désire, il aime jusqu'à souffrir et à mourir; toute beauté l'émeut; rien de ce qui n'est pas beauté ne le touche: " Beauté, dit-il, c'est Vérité; Vérité c'est Beauté. Nous ne savons que cela et n'avons besoin de savior rien autre sur terre! " Nulle action dans ses vers, nulle intention morale. . . .

Indeed the legend still lives. " To admire, to desire, to love, that is what occupied his mind. Only that which is beautiful moved him." Yet it is not strange that a French scholar should fall a victim to the certain blindness that has afflicted so many of Keats's own good countrymen.

But I began by saying that Keats the philosopher is being discovered. It has been no sudden revelation, but rather the gradual evolution of critical impression, which, at first only faintly suggested, has come to be expressed with bold certainty.

Let us note some of the evidence. In the *John Keats Memorial Volume*, published in the Centenary year, 1921, one finds two writers[1] explicitly calling Keats a philosophic poet, a third[2] entitling an article *Keats and " Philosophy*," a fourth devoting three-fourths of his lecture, the most substantial contribution to the volume, to a study of Keats's artistic growth as related to his mental development,[3] a fifth — and I hardly need hint that this is G. B. Shaw, with a sly peek over his spectacles to enjoy the consternation he creates — broadly suggesting that Keats had in him the germs of a bolshevist and that had he lived he might have been a " propagandist and a

[1] a. A. Clutton-Brock: *Keats and Shelley, a Comparison*. b. Arthur Lynch: *John Keats*.
[2] A. C. Bradley.
[3] *The Warton Lecture:* E. de Selincourt.

prophet." [4]   Following the Centenary, came a "Post-Centenary View" from America devoted to proof of the overmastering influence of philosophy in Keats's later life.[5]   And a year later there was published an English volume [6] whose theme is the development of Keats's philosophy from "naturalism" to "idealism"—a book which, though it only imperfectly covers its ground, yet contains many fertile suggestions as to the growth of Keats in mental and artistic power.

But the essays and lectures appearing in the Memorial Volume were not by any means the first indications of a perception of the fact that Keats was a thinker.   The truth began to be apparent when Monckton Milnes, afterwards Lord Houghton, published, in 1848, *The Life, Letters and Literary Remains of John Keats*.   Here was given to the world, along with some fine discriminating critical comment by Mr. Milnes, the first installment of Keats's letters, which, it should be said, form an indispensable clue to an insight into the real Keats. They were not all here; some of the most important ones were not to appear for over half a century,—in Forman's and Colvin's later editions, and now in Amy Lowell's new biography,—but there were enough, together with other testimony from the manuscripts of the poet's contemporaries, to open up an entirely new world to students of Keats.

The first important critical work to pay attention to Keats's ideas was F. M. Owen's *Keats, a Study*, published in 1880. Mrs. Owen's criticism is particularly sympathetic throughout, but is of interest to us in this study chiefly because of hints dropped here and there as to Keats's thought and of a first attempt to trace the allegorical meaning of *Endymion*.   She suggests the possibility of an interpretation of *Endymion* as "Imagination in all time searching for the spirit of Beauty," with Cynthia as the beauty of a bygone age when the world was young, and with the Indian Princess as the representation

[4] *John Keats.*
[5] G. R. Elliott: *The Real Tragedy of Keats*, Publications of The Modern Language Association, 1921, p. 315.
[6] H. I'A. Fausset: *Keats, A Study in Development.*

of the " new phases on which Imagination has entered " —
Imagination having at last discovered " the eternal unity of
all Beauty," and become " one with it forever." But she
thinks there is a larger meaning, and this she develops.
Endymion, she suggests, is the story of the Spirit of man,
which becomes awakened by a higher spiritual power, and
thence begins a quest for the higher spiritual state. This he
eventually reaches, after a series of trials through earth, fire,
and water, by means of which his soul is so schooled as to
learn the one deepest lesson: " that no love is true which
does not realize itself as part of a larger whole — that all that
is beautiful is One." This he discovers when his beloved and
Cynthia are revealed to him as identical, " and he knows that
all love and beauty is one, that the fitful and dimly realized
beauty in common life and the beauty gained through suffering is one with the beauty of light and joy and that it was
necessary that some change should spiritualize him into that
belief." The interpretation is not satisfying, but it is evidence
of what one perceives throughout the study — that the author
has caught fleeting glimpses of thought, usually aesthetic in
nature, in Keats's poems. *Lamia* is the time of " yeasting
youth," when " philosophy is at strife with the enthralment
of the passions "; in the *Ode on a Grecian Urn,* we are told
that the " Past is made alive in these words, its beauty has
never died, and the very material in which the Attic shape is
wrought is infused with life ": all in all, Keats shows us in
this poem that to love Beauty is to love Truth, and that when
we are spiritualized enough to recognize them, both shall
appear to us as one." And so we find, sketched lightly
through or merely suggested, many ideas that have since been
built upon in more detail. There is something original and
stimulating in the author's perspective. It was a pioneer work
in exploring the mind of Keats.

In his *Cobwebs of Criticism,* Hall Caine, a little later, points
out that it is evident " that Keats at one period turned all
his soul to the love of philosophy " and that, though down to

the last, perhaps, " he over-rated the Paradise of Sensation in contrast with the Paradise of the Mind," he was yet " far from indifferent to the problems of human life and destiny." Moreover, there was a moral core in Keats, which might have resulted in his becoming a " great teacher of men," but he lacked the necessary sobriety of temper to realize this. Keats came to understand, too, Mr. Caine says, the truth about dreamers, that it is well for a mere dreamer to learn early that his dreams are useless; but the knowledge came too late. However, Caine does not go on with his leads; he only suggests.

Then in Matthew Arnold's essay, which, in spite of the misleading first two or three pages, is really a great encomium on Keats, we find some advance. Arnold had new evidence to work on, — the new four-volume edition of Keats's letters and poems, by Forman, published 1883, — and he made good use of it. For the most part, the essayist is concerned with a vindication of the character of Keats; but he goes further than that, and comments upon his genius and his central ideas. It is often said that Arnold gives Keats a place beside Shakes-peare; and so, in a limited field, he does. " In one of the two great modes by which poetry interprets, in the faculty of naturalistic interpretation, in what we call natural magic, he ranks with Shakespeare," Arnold declares. And then he adds, more emphatically, making use of a quotation from Keats: " ' I think,' he said humbly, ' I shall be among the English poets after my death.' He is; he is with Shakes-peare." As to Keats's idea of beauty, Arnold remarks: " The truth is that the ' yearning passion for the Beautiful,' which was with Keats, as he himself truly says, the master passion, is not a passion of the sensuous or sentimental poet. It is an intellectual and spiritual passion. It is ' connected and made one,' as Keats declares that in his case it was, ' with the ambi-tion of the intellect.' " With this good start, the master critic leaves us.

A notable criticism in which Keats's ideas and intellect are given some prominence is the well known introduction written by Robert Bridges for the G. Thorn Drury edition of Keats's poems in 1894. Mr. Bridges' judgments are, to say the least, conservative, his praise all nicely balanced by judicial reservations. Yet he recognizes that Keats's mind had a philosophic bent, though he felt it to be more instinctive than reasoned. He is not quite sure, but *Endymion, Lamia,* and *Hyperion* appear to be capable of allegoric interpretation, so he gives his ideas of their meaning for what they are worth, — and, especially in the case of *Endymion,* shows some spirit in doing it. The power to understand or to delineate human passion is a part of Keats's nature. As for his doctrine of beauty, Keats fails to " spiritualize " it; hence it cannot be defended.

I give here a bare suggestion of the interpretation of the *Endymion* that Mr. Bridges offers. " The Moon represents ' Poetry ' or the Ideality of desired objects, *The principle of Beauty in all things:* it is the supersensuous quality which makes all desired objects ideal; and Cynthia, as moon-goddess, crowns and personifies this, representing the ideal beauty or love of woman: and in so far as she is also actually the Moon as well as the Indian lady, — who clearly represents real or sensuous passion, — it follows that the love of woman is in its essence the same with all love of beauty." Man begins with some ambition, say, fame, and connecting " Moon with his passion," he sees " Ideality in his desire." " This Ideality, assuming the form of the goddess, that is, of woman, *which it is,* makes him renounce ambition and pursue poetic love." He must now humanize this passion by contact with tragedy and pain. This sympathy leads him to sensuous passion, which seems in direct conflict with his ideal passion until he discovers they are the same. I should add that the four regions in which the action takes place are " Earth, Fire, Water, and Air."

Mr. Bridges is interestingly suggestive, and though he approaches Keats with his fingers crossed, in general inclining to the traditional side of the question, his essay is one of the most fruitful studies of Keats yet made.

In 1905, Mr. Ernest de Selincourt put out his splendid edition of Keats's poems, with its rare introduction and its sumptuous notes, all breathing of ripe scholarship and patient, devoted care. Mr. de Selincourt has from the first, it seems, been deeply concerned in the intellectual Keats, and has jealously sought to shield his loved poet from possible adverse criticism. Mr. de Selincourt, too, offers an allegorical interpretation of *Endymion* and *Hyperion*, and points out the conflict between reason and emotion in *Lamia;* he contends, and establishes his contention, that the expression " O for a life of Sensations rather than of Thoughts," should not be read literally, but that " Sensations " as used here should be interpreted as imagination or intuitive feeling. He traces certain evidences of the influence of Wordsworth on Keats's thought, successfully, I think, and in that light interprets various passages from both his poems and his letters. Altogether, in the introduction and notes in this volume, we have the clearest approach to the mind of Keats up to this time. But, although we find many acute remarks on some of Keats's characteristic utterances on poetic theory and his philosophy in general, these are not followed up; they usually remain but intimations only. Moreover, Mr. de Selincourt's understanding of Keats's idea of Beauty at this time is close to the traditional one, and is at best merely sketched out.

In Mr. Hancock's agreeable biography of Keats, which appeared in 1908, there are two chapters to which the student looking for comment on Keats's thought turns with anticipation, but reads with disappointment. One is called " Philosophy of His Art," the other, " The Principle of Beauty." But Mr. Hancock only cursorily treats these subjects. The first chapter becomes largely a discussion of the idea that "first in beauty should be first in might," in its implication as to moral conduct, and in the section entitled *The Principle of Beauty,* we are told that Keats's artistic life was parallel to Tennyson's Soul in the *Palace of Art,* except that " great poetry and a passion for length of days " rather than nausea is the result. However, even though Hancock has not gone far with this phase of Keats, he does throw out interesting suggestions. He agrees with Mr. de Selincourt on the meaning of "O for a life of Sensations"; he declares that Keats anticipates Browning in the "healthy humanism in which the flesh helps the soul, and the soul helps the flesh," and he gives as Keats's philosophy in the *Ode on a Grecian Urn,* an interpretation, which, while it probably applies little to the poem in question, does, nevertheless, express a conviction somewhat related to one held by Keats as a condition necessary to all art creation and art appreciation — Schiller's idea of freedom.[7] But to Hancock, Keats " did not see life large." " He passed through the clamor of the times singing, like Horace, his Lalage of beauty." " His message was first in beauty, first in might "; but the author never makes clear just what this *beauty* is.

A minor yet significant contribution to our subject is to be found in Dr. Paul Starick's *Die Belesenheit von John Keats und Die Grundzüge Seiner Literarischen Kritik,* published in Berlin, 1910. This is a doctoral dissertation devoted largely to Keats's literary background as it was built up through reading and study. But under the section entitled *Die Grundzüge Seiner Literarischen Kritik,* Dr. Starick briefly outlines Keats's aesthetic philosophy. The treatment is incomplete, yet the author in one way or another touches upon the majority of Keats's conceptions of what poetry should be, and thereby suggests a more detailed study. Mr. Starick's most distinct service, however, is to point out the similarity

[7] "True art has for its object not merely to afford transient pleasure, to excite a momentary gleam of liberty. Her aim is to make us intrinsically and absolutely free. And this she accomplishes by awakening, exercising and perfecting in us a power to remove to an objective distance the world of the senses — which otherwise only burdens us as a dead weight, as blind force — to transform it into the free working of our spirit and thus to master matter by means of the idea."
Schiller: *The Use of the Chorus in Tragedy.*

between Keats's aesthetic views and those of Hazlitt and
Coleridge, especially as to the high seriousness of poetry and
the fundamental importance of the imagination in creative
work; though this likeness, Mr. Starick explains, rightly I
think, is to be traced less to direct influence than to parallel
thinking on the same subjects. For Keats had read only the
poetry of Coleridge, not his critical works, and, although he
heard Hazlitt's lectures during the winter of 1817–1818, the
young poet's ideas were probably not much altered as a result.
Hazlitt's teachings may have deepened and clarified Keats's
conceptions, but did not materially change them.

In a volume also published in 1910, and entitled *John
Keats, Sa Vie et Son Oeuvre,* Lucien Wolff likewise detects the
philosophic trend in Keats. Though he denies to the poet
interest in life and the great public movements of his day, yet
he credits him with rather important aesthetic ideas. Mr.
Wolff interprets *Endymion* as an allegory, with the shepherd
prince representing Keats himself as a poet in search of the
"supreme beauty of the world " (*beauté suprême du monde*).
The moon is the most perfect beauty of the physical world;
Cynthia or Phoebus is the ideal or the supreme conquest of
humanity. Mr. Wolff fails to preserve a clear-cut definition of
his figures in explaining the allegory, but his general conclusions are distinct: Human affection, manifested through love
for woman and sympathy for humanity, and the ideal loves
are in essence one. An all-desirable goal for the poet is repose;
but " it is necessary to have each of these aspirations, to suffer
for them, and to be spiritualized by them before one can
arrive at the supreme object which reconciles the diverse im-
pulsions of human nature and gives repose." It is the possibility of finding spiritual repose in a work of art, too, that
is celebrated in the *Ode on a Grecian Urn.* Here it is shown
that, subjectively, human sorrow may be vanquished forever
in the conquest of the infinite certitude that " eternal Beauty
and eternal Truth are one." Mr. Wolff also points out Keats's
emphasis on a poet's knowledge of the human heart and an

understanding of the suffering of the world, as set forth in the *Fall of Hyperion* and in certain letters. Yet, in general, this French critic is only incidentally interested in Keats's thought; he is more concerned with the poet's life and an appreciation of his poetry. Consequently, he does not attempt a complete view of his philosophic ideas.

In S. J. Mary Suddard's *Studies and Essays,* written in 1909, but published in 1912, we find in *The Evolution of Keats's Mind* and *Keats's " Prelude "* the first evidence of a systematic attempt to study Keats's mind. But Miss Suddard's outlook is too limited, and the scope of her investigation too confined for entirely satisfactory results. To her, Keats seems too preoccupied with one special form of truth to be deeply concerned with any of the other types. In his eager pursuit of the one aim "beauty in art," he becomes oblivious of the ordinary interests of humanity, and refuses to permit philosophy to hold his attention. The author first sets out to interpret Keats's idea of poetry as revealed in the 1917 volume of poems, incidentally using evidence found in later letters to substantiate her claims. These early poems, especially, constitute Keats's " Prelude." *Sleep and Poetry* reveals his plan for poetic education, how he should first wander through the region of the sensuous, only to pass from that to a higher spiritual realm of interpretation of life. At first, as shown in these poems, Keats " approaches art from the outside through the methods, rather than the spirit of the masters." From nature he expects direct inspiration without giving anything in return. But soon he learns that he must take to nature human emotion and sympathy. " The life he feels in nature is his own." Then, a " subtler feeling steals " upon him, as he understands more of the inner life of the physical world. He sees an inner bond uniting all, " a new organic life," that at once inspires to poetic creation and reveals the " interpenetration of Nature and the soul." So all poetry is " the outcome of an impression produced by Nature." The theory of poetic art evolved is that of " Pleasure as the end," supplemented by " Beauty as the means." In the beginning, it had been enough for Keats simply to give his teeming being self-expression; he failed in adequate ripeness of presentation; but later he learns that he must take the reader into consideration. Now " instead of requiring the reader to accept an alien ideal," he sees that poetry should " set before him his own unconscious ideal incarnate." In order to do this, Keats saw that he must know human psychology, and to know human psychology he must get knowledge and experience; so the author fits to her thesis — that Keats refused to incline his ears to any but the " truth of beauty " — all the facts connected with the poet's eager desire to acquire knowledge, not that he might interpret life better, but that he might speak to the world in its own language.

One cannot go to these essays for an adequate treatment of Keats's views on poetry. The material used is too scanty, and the conclusions often too far-fetched to be of value. Nevertheless, the work is important. No one before had so well pointed out Keats's conscious application of himself to a definite plan of poetic development; no one had before so well interpreted *Sleep and Poetry* in its autobiographical implications.

And now we come to Sidney Colvin's monumental *Life of John Keats*, of 1917. I must not attempt a summary of the ideas as to Keats's thought contained in this volume. They are so many, and so rich and varied that the task would be too great. Not that Colvin makes any systematic attempt to outline Keats's philosophic or aesthetic theories; his chief anxiety is Keats the man and Keats the poet. But he does furnish abundant material for a study of the mind of Keats, and often he goes further: he concurs with de Selincourt and Hancock in their interpretation of " Sensations " as " intuitions of the mind "; he agrees in part with Bridges as to the influence of Wordsworth in *Sleep and Poetry* and the Mansion of Life letter; he furnishes an elaborate analysis of *Endymion* as an allegory, which seems to me to be the most satisfactory interpretation yet advanced; treats *Hyperion* with the same care; interprets *Lamia* as a thought poem; and, altogether, makes many a fruitful excursion into the field of Keats the thinker. But he does not bring home his fruits, does not garner them into a separate storehouse for inspection and classification. What strikes one most is Mr. Colvin's rightness in these many ventures into the mental deeps of Keats. Were he only to speak directly and systematically to the question of Keats's thought, his analysis should be final and conclusive.

As to the meaning of *Endymion,* I can best give a suggestion of Mr. Colvin's interpretation in his own words:

> Let it be borne in mind, then, that besides the fundamental idea of treating the passion of Endymion for Cynthia as a type of the passion of the poetic soul for essential Beauty, Keats wrote under the influence of two secondary moral ideas or convictions, inchoate probably in his mind when he began, but gaining definiteness as he went on. One was that the soul enamoured of and pursuing Beauty cannot achieve its quest in selfishness and isolation, but to succeed must first be taken out of itself and purified by active sympathy with the lives and sufferings of others: the other, that a passion for the manifold separate and individual beauties of things and beings upon earth is in its nature identical with the passion for that transcendental and essential beauty. (*John Keats,* p. 172.)

Mr. Colvin disagrees with Mr. Bridges and Mr. de Selincourt on the question of the Earth, Fire, Water, and Air theory. His interpretation also puts the meaning of the poem on a much more definitely spiritual and aesthetic basis than those preceding. It is, in this respect, on a plane with that penetrative and sympathetic treatment of Keats and his poetry which is the distinctive feature of this great biography.

A later interpretation of *Endymion,* which must be mentioned here, comes from far-away South Africa. Professor H. C. Notcutt, writing in 1919, from the University of Stellenbosh, also explains the poem as an allegory. His explanation is the most elaborate yet advanced; but it differs essentially from others only in that he sees *Endymion* largely as a representation of conflicting ideals in Keats himself — a passionate desire to serve his fellow creatures on one side and longing aspirations after beauty on the other. In the end the poet sees that there is no real conflict here, but these ideals " are one and the same."

As I have said, the *John Keats Memorial Volume* of the 1921 Centenary contained much that bore directly upon the subject of Keats's thinking. There is here no hesitation and no reservation; the authors come out emphatically in their conviction as to Keats's philosophic bent. Mr. Arthur Lynch declares, " ' Keats was a philosopher first, a poet afterwards.' The words are his own, and they strike to the ' white of truth ' in the understanding of his poetry "; and A. Clutton-Brock asserts, " Keats was a philosophic poet, and for that very reason he fell into no philosophic errors in his conception of poetry." Professor Bradley entitles his articles *Keats and " Philosophy,"* and, while he denies to Keats a philosophy in the " strict or technical sense," he interprets the poet's word " philosophy " to mean " such reflection on human nature and life and the world as any thoughtful man may practice; . . . a reflection intent no doubt, but neither technical nor systematic." He longed for advance in it because he hoped it would lighten the burden of the mystery. But neither Mr. Lynch, Mr. Clutton-Brock, nor Mr. Bradley essays to go far into his subject. Mr. Lynch has a new interpretation for certain passages in *Endymion*. It is in *Endymion* that he finds justification for some of the most fulsome praise ever lavished upon Keats. " Keats, a true poet," he exclaims, " becomes something more. He seems the mind the most finely touched, the most deeply inspired by the celestial meaning, of all in the range of literature." *Endymion* he calls a " book of religion," and of Keats's philosophic contribution, he says, " What he has done is to give us beams of illumination, flashes of insight, indications, and aphorisms of genius. To the Greek conception he added something that spoke of motive and purpose, something that responded to the search for an ideal true and ethereal, yet not too remote from the scope of ordinary lives." Mr. Lynch's definition of Keats's " Beauty " is worth quoting:

Truth and beauty were not to Keats the adornments of a high work; they belonged to its inmost spirit. Beauty arises out of the full development in conformity with Nature of a living thing; but in the great All of things the forces that are immortal, that are potent, are not those of immediate violence but those of delicate and tender touch; these respond to our aspirations in the most sensitive moods of vision and thought.

Mr. Clutton-Brock places a high value on the letters. Shelley, he says, could not write in prose, but " Keats could put the whole of himself into a prose sentence as into a line of verse; he felt and thought naturally in prose. . . . And in his letters again and again we see an intellect of the first order expressing itself naturally in prose, with the subtlety, the detachment, of the philosopher." Two more striking statements from Clutton-Brock, I must quote: " Shelley was always making an heroic attempt to live his imaginative life in reality, to make the world what he desired. Keats, on the other hand, began with an aesthetic; and until near the end of his life, it was a principle of that aesthetic that the world of art and the actual world were utterly separate "; and the other, " Poetry . . . was to him a separate state of being in which everything became real; and his aim, as a poet, was to express this reality, to draw everything in its peculiarity, which, he believed, was its beauty."

Mr. Bradley, as I have indicated, shows little interest in the aesthetic philosophy of Keats. But he undertakes to explain Keats's thought on some of the perplexing problems connected with this world of misery and troubles and his attitude toward death. I shall later refer to these ideas in greater detail.

Mr. de Selincourt's Warton Lecture in the Memorial Volume is, as he says, an expansion of what he had written sixteen years earlier. His emphasis on Keats's aesthetic ideas is, however, even more pronounced than before. His problem here is to trace the artistic evolution of the poet. " Keats,"

he says, " is the most striking example of a poet self-educated
and disciplined by his own severe and strenuous effort. His
artistic evolution can be traced step by step, for he continually
reviewed his art in the light of his ideas which grew in acute-
ness, and of his experience which grew in depth and bitter-
ness; . . . he had a mind and spirit bent on applying to his art
the searching test of hard thought and vital experience. We
only read Keats aright when we learn from his own lips that
he wrote, not for art's sake only, but for the sake of truth
and for the sake of life." Such is the tone of Mr. de Selincourt's lecture. He points out Keats's keen realization of a
need for knowledge after the failure of *Endymion;* he explains the expression " that first in beauty shall be first in
might," as a realization on Keats's part that perfect " power
can only spring from knowledge, from the widening of the
mind till it comprehends all intellectual and spiritual experience " — such knowledge as is won " through struggle and
through pain." Keats's decline in 1819, he attributes to a
weakened body and to his passion for Fanny Brawne: he
wore himself out " ' in vain reasonings against the reasonings
of love.' . . . He lacked the physical constitution to react
healthily against the strain of his experience."

In the *Revision of Hyperion* is the cry of a defeated man.
Even as Shelley confesses his failure in *The Triumph of Life,*
so Keats here admits how far he has fallen short of the mark.
Yet de Selincourt holds that at the time of writing the
Revision, Keats was passing through a necessary stage in his
growth to poetic stature. He had before sought to escape the
realities of life, but now he saw that it would be necessary to
grapple with them. " But that stature he did not live to
gain; and lovely as is much that he has left us, we know that
his greatest poetry was still unwritten at his death." It is
clear that had he lived, declares Mr. de Selincourt, " his poetry
. . . would have gained an even firmer hold upon the realities
of human experience." In spite of pessimistic moods, Keats
was ever loyal to poetry. In the *Ode to a Nightingale* he

had taught that man passes, but beauty is immortal; in the *Ode on a Grecian Urn* he had shown that "what Nature does in the eternal resurrection of her loveliness man can achieve by the creative energy of art." In his most fevered days, he could still cry, "Poetry is all I care for, all I live for."

Mr. de Selincourt's lecture is written from the great heart of a sympathetic and attentive critic. On the whole, his conclusions are solid bits of truth sifted from the often elusive evidence before him. The author's limits, however, are fixed by the nature of a lecture, and there is not opportunity to expand and demonstrate. What we really have is a series of large brush strokes that give a general effect without sufficient detail to make the picture clear. Naturally, in the brief space allowed, Mr. de Selincourt has not attempted to treat Keats's aesthetic ideas fully; what he has done is to outline and suggest, to lay a ground-work upon which others may later build.

Mr. G. R. Elliott's *The Real Tragedy of Keats — A Post Centenary View*, which appeared in the Publications of the Modern Language Association for 1921, is arresting, for the reason that it makes philosophy and not love, disease, and poverty the cause of Keats's early death. Mr. Elliott argues that "Nothing is more significant in the Letters than the definitive alteration, within three years, of Keats's attitude to philosophy." Indeed, this change was so radical, according to Mr. Elliott, that there came to be in Keats a definite struggle between philosophy and his art. And it was because these two opposing elements had become obviously irreconcilable that Keats began to crumble. The "real tragedy" then was a hopeless conflict between his "thought" and his native imagination. The overpowering weight of the hopelessness of any reconciliation was what crushed Keats in late 1819; it was not illness, it was not love, the writer maintains, it was the oppressive sense of impotence in facing the necessity for a peace of spirit he could not find. The fact is,

Elliott holds, had Keats lived, he probably could never have escaped the clutches of these conflicting impulses, so could not have gone on in his poetry. In all this, Mr. Elliott is in direct conflict with Mr. de Selincourt, who in his Warton Lecture felt Keats's mental perplexity at the time of writing *The Fall of Hyperion* to be merely an incident in the poet's upward march to greater heights. What Keats sought for, insists Elliott, was supreme repose in poetry and "articulate communion with high truth." In his day he could not attain that: " the scale of human values had become too unsettled to permit of that large certainty of judgment — at its worst, that placid mental conventionalism, — which enabled Shakespeare to watch the struggling spectacle of life with artistic quietude." So Keats sank in the mire of helpless inner conflict, and we find him in *The Cap and Bells* and *The Revision of Hyperion* at grips with his antagonistic impulses — in the first " reaching anxiously for philosophic truth, and stultifying his poetic perception "; in the second, " pulled in the other direction by his instinct for immediate artistic effect." But harmonization of these two forces was impossible, Elliott argues. Keats understood this; hence the " profound pessimism " shown in later letters, which is " fully intelligible only as an exhalation from the real incompetency which had now come over his creative power." " He sought the peace of wisdom; but this being too far above him, his spirit leaned toward the stillness of death."

Mr. Elliott's argument is a mixture of truth and fallacy. Taken in contrast with Mr. de Selincourt's lecture, it demonstrates what plausible argument can be made for or against a proposition, all depending on what evidence the writer selects and emphasizes. It is from such argument that unfortunate legends, based on half truths, grow.

There remains but one more contribution to our subject. This work is also an outgrowth of the Centenary year. It is of special importance for the reason that it is the first complete volume dealing exclusively with Keats's mind ever published. In his *Keats, A Study in Development,* Mr. H. I. 'A. Fausset proposes, to use his own words, " to trace through Keats's poetry, chronologically considered, the stages by which he purified his imaginative insight, by which in fact he advanced from sensationalism to idealism." By " sensationalism," or " naturalism " as he often calls it, Mr. Fausset seems to mean a disposition to live unreflectingly from sensation to sensation, to be steeped in the physical of the world, and to place it first, the spiritual last. " Idealism " seems to be not only the placing of the spiritual first, the sensuous second, but the finding of a purposeful, harmonious unity in the universe. Keats's poetry, declares Mr. Fausset, " reveals an organic unity, to which each particular poem contributes a part, representing a step or a stage in the direction of that absolute goal for which we discover Keats to have been aiming." In the study of the details of Keats's " spiritual development," the author proposes to limit himself to the poems, though he suggests that his conclusions may be doubly reinforced by reference to the letters. However, " the poetry, uncomplicated by notes or circumstantial exegesis, remains as the only ultimate evidence" on the matter. The writer frankly commits himself to a study in which " the philosophic understanding " of Keats's poetry, " the metaphysical problem," hitherto neglected, shall be emphasized.

Mr. Fausset's method is to trace through Keats's poetry, in alleged chronological order, the evidence of his advance in aesthetic insight and in artistic power. He points out how, beginning in *I Stood Tip-Toe* with almost pure " sensationalism," by the time *Sleep and Poetry* is reached, Keats has registered a decided advance toward " idealism." In *I Stood Tip-Toe* there was no real understanding of nature; Keats merely took " languid pleasure in her." But in *Sleep and Poetry,* " he had turned not only to Shakespeare and Wordsworth in literature, but in critical sincerity to Nature herself. There is evident both a profounder if inconsistent consciousness of human values, and a corresponding improvement

in the power and purity of his expression. He had quickly
ceased in fact to see life as an exotic spectacle, women as
nymphs in tapestry, and virtue as the mock chivalry of Calidore. He had realized that poetry implied not pleasurable in-
dulgence but a passionate struggle for truth." He perceived
at this time, too, the antithesis between "naturalism and
idealism."

In *Sleep and Poetry*, Keats was trying to formulate the
"vast idea" of poetry he had apprehended, but he failed. In
Endymion he again attempted to bring this infinite idea into
the realm of consciousness. His method is allegorical interpretation. The advance over *Sleep and Poetry* is "that Keats
has now greatly defined and particularized an idealism which
was previously only a vast intuition." But the net result is
again failure, for the poem proves that Keats "has only advanced to the point where he can speak intimately the language
of human instinct, expressing nature from within in language
rich and excessive as her own vegetation; but that a true
consciousness of her idea still escapes him, in the confusion
of matter which repeatedly overwhelmed his senses." Just as
in the 1817 poems Keats had been unable fully to express his
conception of nature, so here his apprehension of the idea of
life is external, and adequate formulation of its spirit
escapes him.

And so the author goes on through the other poems. In the
Ode to a Nightingale and *On a Grecian Urn*, the "imper-
manence, the discord and the decay of man is contrasted with
a state of existence which Keats visions as eternal and un-
alterable." But it is not the work of art itself which is permanent: " In both cases then, it is the idea of beauty, expressed
through a work of art and a voice of nature, which he con-
trasts with the fact of man." There is here then an emerging
of aesthetic idea, but Keats's weakness, as revealed especially
in the *Ode to a Nightingale*, is that though "he could apprehend truth through pleasure, he could not detect it behind pain
or apparent ugliness."

But in the *Revision of Hyperion,* Mr. Fausset declares, Keats truly finds himself. In the original version his ideas had been vague, but this final poem represents very accurately the philosophical conviction which the poet now possessed. He " has attained at last to the idea, the central reality, into which all the sensations of life are gathered, in which gladness and sorrow, life and death, lose those attributes of contrast conditioned by earth, in which the passion, whether of hatred or of love is soothed and mitigated into a union of benignant light. Good and evil are become one, not in a realistic sur- render of distinction, but in ideal reconcilement, in the liberty of Love."

Mr. Fausset's book contains many single passages of acute critical suggestion. The volume is worth reading for these alone. It is also worth study as an interesting attempt to trace the development of Keats's mind as revealed in his poetry. But the writer fails in the one object he sets out to accomplish: namely, to show from the poems a progressive development in Keats's poetic principles. In the beginning, the writer commits himself to the proposition that " each par- ticular poem contributes a part, representing a step or a stage in the direction of that absolute goal for which we discover Keats to have been aiming." He also promises to establish his case on the evidence of the poems alone.

Now such a project must necessarily fail. It must fail, first, for the reason that the poems in chronological arrangement do not each one in order reveal development in Keats's aesthetic thinking. For instance, *I Stood Tip-Toe,* according to the authority of Mr. Colvin,[8] was written contemporaneously with, or even followed, rather than preceded, *Sleep and Poetry.* Yet Mr. Fausset spends many pages, nearly a tenth of the book in fact, showing Keats's advance from *naturalism* to *idealism* in *Sleep and Poetry* over *I Stood Tip-Toe.*

Other facts do not at all support the hypothesis of a pro-

[8] In *The Poems of John Keats in Chronological Order,* 1917, *Sleep and Poetry* precedes *I Stood Tip-Toe.* — See also Colvin's *John Keats,* p. 115.

gression from poem to poem toward idealism. The argument relative to *Hyperion* is a case in point. *Hyperion,* states Mr. Fausset, is extremely significant for the reason that Keats, " in the act of creating it, forced into the full daylight of his mind the principle upon which he was acting when he wrote *The Eve of St. Agnes* or the *Ode to Autumn,* namely, the submission of the sensations received from nature to the dictatorship of selective reason." This would be progression indeed, but the whole statement loses its force when we recall that the *Ode to Autumn* was written at least six months after [9] the first version was completed, and that *The Eve of St. Agnes* probably followed, was at least written contemporaneously with, *Hyperion.* A further examination of Mr. Fausset's conclusions as to *Hyperion* and *The Eve of St. Agnes* reveals the extent of this odd discrepancy. Of the latter poem he declares: " If Keats's career had ended with the writing of *The Eve of St. Agnes* there would have been every excuse for posterity's acceptance of him as a poet who sought beauty for beauty's sake rather than for truth's." In other words, at the time in which this poem was written, taking his poetry as evidence, Keats would appear to be merely a poet of the sensuous, with no high interest in truth, concerned only with " beauty for beauty's sake," art for the sake of art. But, on the other hand, in reading what Mr. Fausset has to say of *Hyperion,* one discovers that he finds it to contain ideas which should forever absolve its writer from the charge of art for art's sake. The argument of *Hyperion,* he says, is, briefly, that the Kingdom of Earth and of natural law must pass, to be replaced by that of " Spirit and of the ideal reason of Love." The poem expresses a " fine idea of evolutionary necessity." The inspired intelligence of a poet is to use nature's varied forces for the " creation of unadultered beauty, in perpetual harmony with the soul of man, because it satisfies his rational

[9] I accept Colvin's dates in *The Poems of John Keats in Chronological Order* and the *Life.* For *Hyperion,* Colvin gives September–January, 1818–1819; for *The Eve of St. Agnes,* January, February, 1819; for *To Autumn,* September, 1819.

as well as his sensuous perception." In *Hyperion,* Keats had perceived that a poet's business is to resolve discord into harmony, " to substitute a world of pure intelligence for one of pure force."

Surely, a poet who believes all this could not at the time be considered one who cared for " beauty for beauty's sake " only. The argument for progression here goes limping fearfully; obviously, there was no distinct change in Keats's aesthetic or philosophic theory from the time of the first version of *Hyperion* to that of the *Eve of St. Agnes;* could not be, unless like a crab the poet had walked backward. *Hyperion* and *St. Agnes Eve* were written in the same period; whatever theories Keats held when he wrote the one, he must have held when he wrote the other.

I might go on, but has not Mr. Fausset himself by his own testimony shown his theory of progressive advancement to be fallacious? Has he not really admitted, what is indubitably true, that in this matter of " naturalism " and " idealism, — taking the author's own definition — Keats's poetry shows advance and recoil, progress and reaction and interaction, an irregular pendulum-like movement, with first one in the ascendancy, then the other?

And that brings me to the second difficulty Mr. Fausset faced, that is, his attempt to make the poems alone tell the story of the development of Keats's mind. Now it is pretty well agreed that if one is to get a clear conception of the growth of Keats's ideas on his art, one must go to his letters, studying them together with the poems. A study of the poems in chronological order will indicate Keats's advance in poetic capacity, in power of adequate expression, in self-restraint, but not in ideas of his art. That Mr. Fausset at least unconsciously felt this to be the case is witnessed by this sentence from his discussion: " When . . . he turned to write *The Fall of Hyperion,* he had for the first time made the idea which had so long vaguely eluded him sufficiently his own to demand a directer expression." The facts are, though, that there is almost noth-

ing new said in the *Revision of Hyperion* that had not already
been expressed before, chiefly in letters. But, unfortunately,
Mr. Fausset does not make consistent use of Keats's correspondence, and therefore does not show this. Perhaps it is in
this failure to use the letters that Mr. Fausset makes his chief
mistake. The difficulty in the plan of omitting the correspondence in any study of Keats's mind, and especially in a
study of his poetic ideas, is that the findings must necessarily
be incomplete. Whole fields of rich suggestion in this case
remain unplowed, and the harvest must necessarily be to that
extent scanty.

Consequently, as a treatise on Keats's aesthetic, it must be
confessed Mr. Fausset's book is not all a success. Valuable
suggestion and interpretation it contains, but if one is looking
for a complete, impartial study of the subject, in which all
the available facts are marshalled and analyzed, and from
them conclusions drawn without regard to the support or de-
nial of any preconceived thesis, one will not find it here. In
the final analysis, Mr. Fausset's study becomes more valuable
as an examination of Keats's development of capacity to say
what he had to say than a revelation of the growth of the
theories of his art.

II

It is not remarkable that keen and sympathetic critics have
of late been turning their attention to the thought side of
Keats; the only wonder is that the movement has been so
long delayed. For any thorough study of the poems and
letters must end in the conviction that Keats was at core a
thinker, and not merely a poet of the sensuous and lovely
whose eye saw no deeper than the mere surface of things.
Contrary to widely accepted opinion, he took a keen interest
in, and showed profound insight into, the life about him, the
evidence for which, when gathered together, is astonishing;
he had a philosophy of life, balanced, sane, and in many re-

spects, profound; and, finally, he had an aesthetic philosophy
— into which all his thinking eventually converged — that included striking theories upon most of the fundamental problems of poetry.

A candid scrutiny of available evidence must convince the
most sceptical that Keats cannot be regarded as an unconscious artist, — if there be any such, — but as one who studied
his art with eyes wide open, and, so far as power lay within
him, molded his verse to fit his ideals. Almost from the first
he was thinking hard on the nature of poetry and the poetic
art. Of the thirteen poems, exclusive of the sonnets, in the
1817 volume, seven have to do either all or in part with
poetic theory. In one of his earliest letters extant is contained the sonnet beginning " Great spirits now on earth are
sojourning " in which he declares his faith in Wordsworth,
Hunt, and Haydon [10] as agents in the regeneration of poetry —
" these will give the world another heart." Indeed, it is probable that had Keats concerned himself less with theory and
" philosophy " in his early days, his poems would have been
better understood and infinitely more appreciated. We have
been recently told again that Keats " had no moral purpose in
his work." [11] Yet his letters and his poems bear constant
testimony to the fact that he almost continually wrestled
with the most elusive problems of life; and he wrote hardly an
important poem that is not charged with more or less preg-
nant suggestions and reasoning on the nature and purpose of
poetry. One finds this in the poem that heads the list in the
1817 volume; it is in *The Fall of Hyperion*, the last serious
piece he ever wrote. *Lamia*, the *Ode to a Nightingale*,
Endymion, are filled with it; evidence of it may be found in
a dozen of his sonnets and fragments; it even dominates that
well-nigh perfect piece of artistry *Ode on a Grecian Urn*, to
say nothing of the testimony of the letters, which are rich with

[10] *I Stood Tip-Toe* (all), *Sleep and Poetry* (all), *To My Brother George*
(all), *To Felton Mathew* (all), *To Charles Cowden Clarke* (all), *Calidore*
(in part), *Specimen of Induction* (in part).
[11] Jusserand: *Histoire de la Littérature Anglaise*, p. 242.

significant comment on aesthetic problems, forming, as Sidney Colvin says, "one of the most perfect commentaries on a poetic life on record."

And yet the reader must not expect to find in Keats's views on poetry any technical or scientific aesthetic philosophy. Keats never professed a systematic aesthetic; he never put his thought into a formal essay. "What he has done," to borrow the words of Mr. Lynch, used with reference to *Endymion*, "is to give us beams of illumination, flashes of insight, indications and aphorisms of genius." And as I study his works and come to apprehend better the significance of these many beams of illumination and flashes of insight given forth with all the freshness and spontaneity of unpremeditated utterance, the conviction grows upon me that Keats had developed aesthetic theories that should give him rank with Horace, Dante, Wordsworth, Goethe, Schiller, and the rest of that brilliant galaxy of geniuses who not only had ideas of what poetry ought to be, but had the power and skill to compose it in forms of truth and enduring beauty.

The best proof as to the authenticity and value of this aesthetic thinking is probably to be found in its effects on Keats's own poetry. It is safe to say that no other English poet has shown such remarkable advance in artistic power and self restraint as did Keats within the brief working years of his life. It is a little difficult to assign any one definite cause for this unusual growth, but it would seem certain that much of it came as a result of the earnest, even feverish, struggle for clear thinking on the tormenting problems of the poetic art that continually went on in his mind. His confession to Leigh Hunt, "I went to the Isle of Wight, thought so much about poetry so long together, that I could not get to sleep at night; . . . I was too much in solitude, and consequently was obliged to be in continual burning of thought," gives a clue to the intensity with which he wrestled for clear vision. From the purging fires of such thinking emerged a taste ever more and more refined as the dross of immaturity and error was burned away.

The splendid 1819 poems were the fruit of years of intense, even agonized effort to master the principles of poetic art. It would appear that after the failure of *Endymion* there began to take place in the mind of Keats a clarification process in which the eternal facts of poetry in their relation to life were to have proper perspective. Through the year 1818, he was studying, meditating, thinking, — refining his spirit by sitting anew at the feet of Spenser, Shakespeare, Wordsworth, and Milton, steadying his intellect through contact with Hazlitt, above all, schooling his critical taste through the most severe self-analysis, as he sat in stern judgment on his own *Endymion*, pronouncing the work " slip-shod " and full of faults, the product of youthful immaturity, with the final brave, sad sentence, " It is just that this youngster should die away." By January, 1819, there was the beginning of a new light. It was merely a glimmer through the darkness of unsparing " domestic criticism "; but it pointed the way to a clearer view. To Haydon, he writes:

I have been writing a little now and then lately: but nothing to speak of — being discontented and as it were moulting. Yet I do not think I shall ever come to the rope or the Pistol, for after a day or two's melancholy, although I smoke more and more my own insufficiency — I see by little and little more of what is to be done, and how it is to be done should I ever be able to do it. On my soul, there should be some reward for that continual " agonie ennuyeuse."

Haydon's reply, in view of the glorious outburst which produced the 1819 poems, was almost prophetic:

The " agonie ennuyeuse " you talk of be assured is nothing but the intense searching of a glorious spirit, and the disappointment it feels at its first contact with the muddy world — but it will go off — and bye and bye you will shine through it with " fresh Argent."

And indeed Keats did shine through with " fresh argent," in all the immortal poems of the spring of 1819 — the *Eve of St.*

Agnes, the *Ode to a Nightingale,* the *Ode to Psyche,* and the *Ode on a Grecian Urn.* Then came another period of meditation in calm analysis of his mental experiences. Evidently, he has been moulting once more:

> I have great hopes of success, because I make use of my judgment more deliberately than I have yet done; but in case of failure with the world, I shall find my content. . . . I have spent too many thoughtful days and moralized through too many nights for that, and fruitless would they be indeed, if they did not by degrees make me look upon the affairs of the world with a healthy deliberation. . . . I have of late been moulting: not for fresh feathers and wings: they are gone, and in their stead I hope to have a pair of patient sublunary legs. I have altered, not from a chrysalis into a butterfly, but the contrary; having two little loopholes, whence I may look out into the stage of the world: and that world on our coming here I almost forgot.

Thinking through thoughtful days and moralizing through wakeful nights — what were the results of all this meditation? It is that I would show, so far as this thinking had to do with poetry, in the pages that are to follow. It is my immediate problem in this book to discover Keats's leading aesthetic ideas. I propose to bring together from all his writings his most significant utterances on the poetic art, and by analysis and interpretation of these to make clear what he believed.

In beginning this study I was faced by three possibilities: First, to consider in detail all that Keats has said on the theory of his art; second, to study the growth of his ideas throughout the period of his poetic development; third, to treat rather fully his principal theories, subordinating those of a slighter and more transient nature. After study and reflection I settled upon the last method as the one most likely to yield satisfactory results. The first I discarded as impracticable. Keats throws out suggestions here and there quite unrelated to anything else he says; some of his theories he held to the end, others he abandoned almost as soon as they were announced. To deal with all of these as of equal importance would plainly be illogical. The second method offers attractions: Keats did show remarkable mental development in the short span of years allotted him for his working life; but when one comes to consider his aesthetic ideas, it soon becomes apparent that practically all his main theories are uncovered very early; these ripen and mature as time passes, to be sure; they unfold into clearer definition and completer significance; Keats learns to give them fitter, more adequate expression: but in essential quality they remain the same. A study of Mr. Fausset's book, for instance, will show that the author has admitted in one way or another that by the time *Endymion* was finished Keats had outlined most of the essential features of his belief. Mr. Fausset's contention, that Keats did not know what he was saying and did not know how to express in poetry what he wanted to say, does not alter the fact that he actually believed these things at the time.

Moreover, as I have pointed out in my discussion of Mr. Fausset's thesis, there is not a steady progression and development in Keats's aesthetic ideas. It is evident that throughout his poetic career Keats was engaged in a continual intellectual struggle with himself as to the true nature and end of poetry. It began with his first productive period, as a study of the 1817 volume unmistakably proves: *Sleep and Poetry,* especially, records an impassioned dispute between the instinctive, sensuous-loving side of Keats's nature, which delighted in Fancy and the luxurious, and the sterner, deeper, more thoughtful self that saw in the poetic life a consecration to the heart of humanity and to truth. The conflict went on even to the last. In November, 1819, only a month before he gave over all serious writing, he is saying, " As the marvellous is the most enticing and the surest guarantee of harmonious numbers I have been endeavoring to persuade myself to untether Fancy and let her manage for herself. I and myself cannot agree about this at all."

The source of this disagreement lay within Keats's own dual nature. Keats has been called an Elizabethan born out of his time. But the fact is, he is not an Elizabethan any more than he is a Romanticist, or a Greek. In him fate had so wrought as to produce a nature akin to the great elemental geniuses of all times — to Homer, Shakespeare, Dante, to Chaucer, Spenser, Wordsworth. In him was that youthful naïveté that belongs to the childhood of all races; but no less instinctive was that more grown-up yearning passion to know and understand the human heart. If he stood in simple wonder in the presence of nature and sensuous beauty, he was no less enthralled by the eager pursuit of the mystery of life. His native instincts led him as a lad straight to the heart of Greek mythology, and carried him with the same unerring aim into the center of Spenser's realms of beauty and delight; but with like power, instincts no less his own drove him to the real world of men, of Schiller's dramas, of Wordsworth's pastorals, and Shakespeare's tragedies, to the ideal world of Plato, Hegel, and Shelley.

This being true, there could not fail to be a clash, and a clash there was. The opposing elements in Keats's nature demanded reconciliation. The young Parnassian, instinctively feeling himself endowed beyond the portion of ordinary poets, yet withal confused by the very richness and profusion of his gifts, bravely strove to master himself, to bring the mighty impulses of his being into harmony, that all might sing in tune.

And as the months went on Keats often found partial means of reconciliation, but his life was too brief for a consummation of the task, and he died with many vexing problems still unsolved. In practise he had not even progressed so far as in theory. As was natural, the sensuous genius in him developed in advance of the philosophic, and it ever strove for complete mastery, even while Keats sought earnestly to repress it in order to give the sterner, more robust impulses full sway. So, sometimes one self was in the ascendancy, sometimes another. The result of this is that one does not find in Keats's utterances on the poetic art a consecutive, chronological development. What one does find is not an advance from Greek

" naturalism " to Romantic " idealism," such as Mr. Fausset has tried to prove took place in his thinking, but, rather, progress toward a reconciliation between the Greek, the Elizabethan, and the Romantic-philosophic demands into such a harmony as would give each its place in a new, glorious type of poetic nature.[12] But enough to say that because the facts are as they are, I rejected the possibility of treating Keats's aesthetic purely from the point of view of development, and chose the more feasible plan of outlining the main trend of his thought, with reference, however, wherever possible to chronological evolution.

As I proceed with this study I shall reveal the facts as to Keats's beliefs as I have found them. From the material I have been able to gather I shall present my findings as to the young poet's views on certain definite problems that seemed to concern him most, and shall indicate, as specifically as I can, the conclusions to which he had arrived at the time of his death. My aim is to attempt that which as yet has not been done — to bring Keats's aesthetic ideas together into some coherent whole, to weave the scattered, tenuous threads of his thought into some tangible pattern. If in doing this I can present to my readers a vision of a more real and serious Keats in place of the " versifying pet lamb " of tradition I shall feel that my efforts have been richly rewarded.

[12] Note his own words:
" Then I should be most enviable — with the yearning Passion I have for the beautiful, connected and made one with the ambition of my intellect."
— To George and Georgiana Keats. Oct., 1818. Forman, Vol. IV. 187. (All references to Forman in this volume are to the 1901 edition of *The Complete Works of John Keats*. The older Library Edition is now out of print, and is consequently inaccessible to many readers.)

CHAPTER II

THE DREAM WORLD AND THE ACTUAL — AN ANTITHESIS

" Do you know what it is," once said M. de Lamennais, " which makes a man the most suffering of all creatures? It is that he has one foot in the finite and the other in the infinite, and that he is torn asunder, not by four horses as in the horrible old times, but between two worlds." With some modification these words might be taken as descriptive of the aesthetic schism in Keats to which I have referred in my last chapter. The difference is that Keats was not finally torn asunder between the two worlds, but on the contrary, in spite of the sharp divergence in widely separated poles of his thought, he had even during his short life progressed far toward a reconciliation between these opposing claims.

As I have already indicated, there was one side of Keats that demanded, as a condition for poetic creation, a state of detachment in an imaginative flight into a dream world quite separated from actuality; there was another side that insisted that the world of reality, of men and women and pain and sorrow, must have first place in all great poetry. Closely allied and corollary to this was the conflict between the claims of feeling, mere intuition or sensation, and those of thought, reason, and knowledge.

A study of Keats's aesthetic leads us directly to a consideration of these antithetical elements in his nature, and to his progress toward their reconciliation. A discussion of what Keats's general philosophic ideas were I shall reserve for another chapter; I am here concerned with his struggles to find a place in his poetic world for both dreams and actualities, and with his progress toward a solution of this problem. I say " progress toward " because I doubt if he ever felt fully satisfied in his own mind as to how the adjustment could take place; in some of his utterances we see that which points to a near solution, but probably it was never complete, for it would seem from his poems that the conflict between the half of him that longed to luxuriate in Fancy's pleasant realms and the sterner philosophic half that demanded a curb and bridle for the prancing steeds of his imagination, continued to the end.

In one of Keats's comments on Milton's *Paradise Lost* he admirably states as true of Milton's genius the antithesis which he must have recognized in his own.

The genius of Milton,[1] more particularly in respect to its span of immensity, calculated him, by a sort of birthright, for such an " argument " as the Paradise Lost: he had an exquisite passion for what is properly, in the sense of ease and pleasure, poetical Luxury; and with that it appears to me he would fain have been content, if he could, so doing, have preserved his self-respect and feel of duty performed, but there was working in him as it were that same sort of thing as operates in the great world to the end of a Prophecy's being accomplished: therefore he devoted himself rather to the ardours than the pleasures of Song, solacing himself at intervals with cups of old wine; and those are with some exceptions the finest parts of the poem. With some exceptions — for the spirit of mounting and adventure can never be unfruitful or unrewarded: had he not broken through the clouds which envelope so deliciously the Elysian field of verse, and committed himself to the Extreme, we should never have seen Satan as described —

> " But his face
> Deep scars of thunder had entrenched, &c."

This expresses concisely the dual elements in Keats's nature of which we have been talking.[2] He too loved the poetical luxury of mounting and adventure; the "pleasures of song"

[1] Reprinted by H. Buxton Forman in *The Complete Works of John Keats* (1901), Vol. III, p. 256. First published in *The Dial*, April, 1843, in a memoir of George Keats. The notes occurred on a fly-leaf of Keats's copy of Milton, inscribed to Mrs. Dilke.

[2] R. D. Havens, in his *Influence of Milton on English Poets*, suggests a similar idea. pp. 213, 214.

were dear to him and drew him like a polar magnet to the expanses of the poetic dream world, but the more severe and deeper self in him required that the "ardours" of verse too should have their due: that, even though a poet's head may float in the clouds, his feet must be firmly planted on the ground; that the world of thought and actuality must be carried into any poetry of such magnitude as to entitle its writer to a place among the great poets after his death.[3]

Plenty of writers have seen the first quality in Keats plainly, but the pity is they have seen it to the exclusion of all else. Thus, when critics like A. Clutton-Block declare that, for Keats, "the aesthetic life was an escape," that the "aesthetic dream life which he separated so sharply from the actual world was to him more desirable just because it was more individual in all its particulars," that Keats "began with an aesthetic; and until near the end of his life, it was a principle of that aesthetic that the world of art and the actual world were utterly separated," we know that they have failed to see the other side of Keats, that they are not taking into consideration the fact that very early he saw that the capacity for a close and inimate touch with life was quite as vital a part of the poet's equipment as his power to build an ideal dream world for himself.

The facts are, we find in Keats both an early, immature notion of detachment and a later, more developed conception that correspond roughly to an early and a later theory of the typical aesthetic experience. The first showed its beginnings in a young instinct for aesthetic escape. The second grew out of long attempts to reconcile the opposing demands of the dream world and the world of reality. It found its realization in a subjective activity which, though removed from, and independent of, the distractions of the world of reality, yet owes its richness and validity to a conception of life ab-

---

[3] "I think I shall be among the English Poets after my death." To George and Georgiana Keats. Oct., 1818. Forman. Vol. III. p. 176.

stracted from that world through intimate acquaintance with actuality and the human heart.

That the poet or artist must get outside of, or rise above, things of the actual world in his moments of inspiration was from the first almost axiomatic with Keats. The moment of insight with him was a moment of complete emotional absorption, in which the poet lost even his own sense of being in intense pursuit of his imaginative quarry. The extreme of this activity was flight far away from the fret and fever of life into a realm of imaginative delight, into a region of abstractions of the poet's own creation.

It is this sort of experience Keats has in mind when he writes, " But this morning Poetry has conquered, and I have lapsed into those abstractions which are my only life." For by " those abstractions " it seems he does not mean periods of absorption in abstract thinking in the ordinary sense of the term, as one might suppose. Keats could think in this way, as we shall see when we come to study his ideas of life and the " Mystery "; but in connection with poetry and art he meant something different. This is proved by his use of the word " abstract " in other places. In speaking of " the mighty abstract Idea of Beauty," Keats goes on to explain, " I feel more and more every day, as my imagination strengthens, that I do not live in this world alone but in a thousand worlds. No sooner am I alone than shapes of epic greatness are stationed around me, and serve my Spirit the office which is equivalent to a King's body-guard — then ' Tragedy with sceptered pall comes sweeping by.' According to my state of mind I am with Achilles shouting in the Trenches, or with Theocritus in the Vales of Sicily. Or I throw my whole being into Troilus, and repeating those lines, ' I wander like a lost Soul upon the Stygian Banks staying for waftage,' I melt into the air with a voluptuousness so delicate that I am content to be alone." The world of the abstractions here is distinctly an imaginative real of the concrete, peopled by figures from the heroic past and by shapes of epic greatness from the glorious literature of all time. It is to this kind of experience the poet has reference when he says, " When I am in a room with people, if I am ever free from speculating on creations of my own brain, then, not myself goes home to myself, but the identity of every one in the room begins to press upon me, . . ." Speculating on the creations of his own brain carries him into this world of abstractions. Writing to Haydon on the subject of painting, Keats throws out a suggestion that further helps us to understand his meaning of the word " abstract ": " . . . for when a Schoolboy the abstract Idea I had of an heroic painting — was what I cannot describe. I saw it somewhat sideways, large, prominent, round, and color'd with magnificence — somewhat like the feel I have of Anthony and Cleopatra. Or of Alcibiades leaning on his Crimson Couch in his Galley, his broad shoulders imperceptibly heaving with the Sea. That [4] passage in Shakespeare is finer than this — ' See how the surly Warwick mans the wall.' "

So it is apparent that when we recall Keats's expressions as to the abstract we should remember he is using the term in a very special sense as applied to his own imaginative experiences. These periods of abstraction are nothing more nor less than poetic flights into dream-worlds, where the soul of the poet is detached temporarily from the actuality of men and things, and builds for itself a habitation of its own. There was a side of Keats that demanded this type of poetic detachment to the exclusion of all else. What he seemed to feel was that supreme artistic experience could be possible only by such a flight or an elevation of spirit as would free the mind and eye from the entanglements and limitations of earthly realities. In the early poems we observe this idea in its immaturity. Here high poetic experience is described as a sort of ecstatic trance in which the poet flies from reality into an ideal region of romance and love. This conception is most adequately expressed in the epistle *To My Brother George,* and in *I Stood Tip-Toe.* In the first, Keats explains:

---

[4] This should probably read, " What passage in Shakespeare," etc.

> But there are times, when those that love the bay,
> Fly from all sorrowing far, far away;
> A sudden glow comes on them, naught they see
> In water, earth, or air, but poesy.
>
> (ll. 19–22.)

It is " when a poet is in such a trance " that he sees in the air " white coursers paw, and prance," each " bestridden of gay knights," who, at the sound of a warder's trumpet — whose tones reach only the poet's ear, — glide out of " enchanted portals " and tilt in playful quarrel. Beyond these magic portals, " open wide,"

> The Poet's eye can reach those golden halls,
> And view the glory of their festivals;
> Their ladies fair, that in the distance seem
> Fit for the silv'ring of a seraph's dream;
>
> (ll. 35–38.)

In *I Stood Tip-Toe,* nature furnishes the inspiration, is the gateway, to poetic perception. The magic effects of contact with nature are such that

> . . . we feel uplifted from the world,
> Walking upon the white clouds, wreath'd and curl'd.
>
> (ll. 139–140.)

The poet's mind is whirled away from the things of sense and loses itself in imaginative creation. It is in this state of tranced abstraction that there will come to the poet

> Shapes from the invisible world, unearthly singing,
> From out the middle air, from flowery nests,
> And from the pillowy silkiness that rests
> Full in the speculation of the stars.
>
> (ll. 186–189.)

In this manner Keats conceives the old mythological poetry to have been created. A condition for poetical activity is a soaring away from sensible reality. Thus in *To My Brother George,* the poet exclaims:

Fair world, adieu!
Thy dales, and hills, are fading from my view:
Swiftly I mount, upon wide-spreading pinions,
Far from the narrow bounds of thy dominions.
(ll. 103–106.)

These extracts hardly need comment. Discounting a little for playfulness in the epistle to George, they probably stand as a fairly clear expression of the young poet's ideas of the quality of detachment. They belong to a period when, though Keats dimly perceived his goal and knew the general direction he must follow, he had not yet distinguished the particular road he must take to reach it. His unschooled instinct seized upon the method that seemed most obvious — a form of " direct divination." Simply let the fancy roam ; give reins to the steed of imagination to soar away from the earth, to " paw up against the light " ; let the self be lost in an ecstatic trance : whatever is then visible to the inward eye is fit material for high poetry.

There was to come a time when Keats should see clearly what one half of him felt from the first, that mere dreaming in this manner could not make a poet, yet he always adhered to his belief in some form of detachment ; and we see evidence of his conception of poetic experience as a state of detached imaginative flight throughout his work. We find it in *Endymion,* where the poet gets his glimpse of the ideal in a vision, where the poet's stages of progression are described as a losing of his self in various essences, and where most of the chief events take place in a thoroughly other-world atmosphere ; it is to be seen in the *Ode to Indolence,* wherein the poet's mind is described as in a state of tranced abstraction ; it is evident in *The Fall of Hyperion,* which is written as a vision, and in which a magic draught removes the poet from the world of reality ; while there is no better expression of it anywhere than in the second, third and fourth stanzas of the *Ode to a Nightingale,* finally all centered in the lines :

That I might drink, and leave the world unseen,
   And with thee fade away into the forest dim:

Fade far away, dissolve, and quite forget
   What thou among the leaves hast never known,
The weariness, the fever, and the fret
   Here, where men sit and hear each other groan;
Where palsy shakes a few, sad, last gray hairs,
   Where youth grows pale, and spectre-thin, and dies;
Where but to think is to be full of sorrow
   And leaden-eyed despairs,
Where Beauty cannot keep her lustrous eyes,
   Or new Love pine at them beyond to-morrow.

Away! away, for I will fly to thee,
   Not charioted by Bacchus and his pards,
But on the viewless wings of Poesy,
   Though the dull brain perplexes and retards:
Already with thee! tender is the night,
   And haply the Queen-Moon is on her throne,
Cluster'd around by all her starry Fays;

There is present here an expression of a longing to escape
from the world of pain and trouble to a haven of refuge in the
realm of the aesthetic. There is something too of a return to
the earliest form of the trance-like ecstasy, but it is a soberer,
more conscious soaring, which, withal, takes the very world
it is trying to flee along with it; therefore, the poem exhales
a breath of intense mortality and presents a vision of life on
earth and an intuition of the larger world behind. It belongs
to a period when Keats had arrived at a near reconciliation
between his desire for the luxurious in song and his urge
toward a close identity with man and an understanding of
nature and the world.

The other side to this antithesis, the disturbing conviction
that dreams are not enough, but that the poet must concern
himself with the realities of the world in which he is living,
finds expression early in Keats's poetry. But at first its demands seem feeble enough, and connected with the imagina-

tive " luxuries " rather than with the " ardours of song." Thus in the early epistle *To George Felton Mathew,* after dwelling in a somewhat ecstatic vein on the fanciful pleasures of poetry under the inspiration of nature, he invokes the aid of Mathew in finding

> . . . a place where I may greet the maid —
> Where we may soft humanity put on.

Here they should " sit, and rhyme and think on Chatterton " and the " warm-hearted Shakespeare,"

> And thou shouldst moralize on Milton's blindness,
> And mourn the fearful dearth of human kindness
> To those who strove with the bright golden wing
> Of genius, to flap away each sting
> Thrown by the pitiless world.

Not only the lives and fortunes of poets, but the spirit and deeds of patriots should be dwelt upon:

> . . . We next could tell
> Of those who in the cause of freedom fell;
> Of our own Alfred, of Helvetian Tell;
> Of him whose name to every heart's a solace,
> High-minded and unbending William Wallace.

In *To My Brother George,* following the lines portraying the blisses of the ecstatic trance-like experience, is a passage in which Keats describes the more serious work of a poet:

> What though I leave this dull and earthly mould,
> Yet shall my spirit lofty converse hold
> With after times. — The patriot shall feel
> My stern alarum, and unsheath his steel;
> Or, in the senate thunder out my numbers
> To startle princes from their easy slumbers.
> The sage will mingle with each moral theme
> My happy thoughts sententious;
>
> (ll. 71–78.)

And so on for twenty-five more lines.

In *Sleep and Poetry,* finished late in 1816, the claims of the real world are emphatically and unmistakably asserted. The poet has been again describing the rapturous delights of revelling in the fanciful and sensuous realm of " Flora and Old Pan,"

> And can I ever bid these joys farewell?

he asks. The answer is clear and decisive:

> Yes, I must pass them for a nobler life,
> Where I may find the agonies, the strife
> Of human hearts:
>
> (ll. 123–125.)

This is a creed to which Keats adhered to the end. It is noteworthy that in this 1816 poem, belonging to a period when Keats's reflective self is just beginning to awaken, he should announce a theory that in *The Fall of Hyperion*,[5] coming at the crest of his thought life, the last serious poem he ever wrote, he is solemnly reiterating with tenfold emphasis. The poet, he is declaring, must know and understand the human heart, particularly its deepest and most painful experiences. The poetic aspirant in *The Fall of Hyperion* would reach the very " penetralium of the mystery," the height of poetic insight; Moneta explains the one way:

> " None can usurp this height," returned that shade,
> " But those to whom the miseries of the world
> Are misery, and will not let them rest."
>
> (Book I, ll. 147–149.)

The height is the lofty altar of poetic achievement, where the " Mystery " is to be revealed. Only those can reach the goal who have genuinely known the great suffering heart of humanity, who have not only perceived, but have felt as a deep personal pain the dead weight of men's misery.

[5] According to the authority of Sidney Colvin and Ernest de Selincourt, most of this poem, a revision of the earlier *Hyperion*, was written in November and December of 1819. In her recent biography of Keats, Miss Amy Lowell, however, contends that it was begun in 1818, before the *Hyperion*. Miss Lowell's evidence is ingenious and is in part convincing; but even granting her contention as established, her arguments would apply only to small sections of the revision, and not to the main substance of the poem, with which we are here concerned.

Never did Keats voice this conviction more eloquently than in a letter to Miss Jeffrey written six months before the *Hyperion* passage. To use one of Keats's own phrases, some of the expressions in this letter " have rung through my head like a chime a mending." How intense is that characterization of our English poets, as " miserable and mighty poets of the human heart "! How vividly does one's imagination fly in quick sympathy to the Samuel Johnsons, the Thomsons, the Chattertons, of the family of great poets whom the " English world has ill-treated," who have been " trampled aside into the by-paths of life! "

Under the pressure of low finances, Keats had been considering the possibility of shipping as a surgeon's apprentice on board a vessel engaged in Indian trade. He writes:

Your advice about the Indiaman is a very wise advice, because it just suits me, though you are a little in the wrong concerning its destroying the energies of Mind: on the contrary it would be the finest thing in the world to strengthen them — To be thrown among people who care not for you, with whom you have no sympathies, forces the Mind upon its own resources, and leaves it free to make its speculations of the differences of human character and to class them with the calmness of a Botanist.[6] An Indiaman is a little world. One of the great reasons that the English have produced the finest writers in the world is, that the English world has ill-treated them during their lives and foster'd them after their deaths.[7] They have in general been trampled aside into the bye paths of life and seen the festerings of Society. They have not been treated like the Raphaels of Italy. And where is the Englishman and Poet who has given a magnificent Entertainment at the christening of one of his Hero's Horses as Boyardo did? He had a castle in the Appenine. He was a noble Poet of

[6] Again the idea of detached contemplation.
[7] How keenly the sense of the unhappy and tragic lives of these poets weighed upon Keats's own spirit is shown in his almost sobbing confession of what he felt in visiting the home and tomb of Burns: " One song of Burns's is of more worth to you than all I could think for a whole year in his native country. His Misery is a dead weight upon the nimbleness of one's quill — I tried to forget it — to drink toddy without any Care — to write a merry sonnet — it won't do — he talked with Bitches — he drank with blackguards, he was miserable. We can see horribly clear, in the works of such a Man his whole life, as if we were God's spies."
— To Reynolds, July, 1818. Forman. Vol. IV, p. 131.

Romance; not a miserable and mighty Poet of the human Heart. The middle age of Shakespeare was all clouded over; his days were not more happy than Hamlet's who is perhaps more like Shakespeare himself in his common every day Life than any other of his Characters — Ben Johnson was a common Soldier and in the Low countries, in the face of two armies, fought a single combat with a french Trooper and slew him — For all this I will not go on board an Indiaman, nor for example's sake run my head into dark alleys: I dare say my discipline is to come, and plenty of it too. I have been very idle lately, very averse to writing; both from the overpowering idea of our dead poets and from abatement of my love of fame. I hope I am a little more of a Philosopher than I was, consequently a little less of a versifying Pet-lamb.

What more vivid proof of Keats's idea as to the kind of stuff out of which real poetic fibre is made! No second-hand, vicarious sympathy will do. The creation of great poetry demands actual knowledge of the world. The finest poets are made by being trampled into the by-paths of life, where they see with unveiled eyes the " festerings of society "; thus only may one become " a miserable and mighty poet of the human heart." It is an unusual utterance, perhaps one of the truest and most profound remarks on poetry ever made.

Even more decisive is the testimony in the famous letter to Reynolds of May, 1818. Because of its close bearing on many of Keats's poetic theories I shall have occasion to refer to this frequently throughout this book, and shall therefore designate it for the sake of convenience, The Mansion of Life letter. Keats's conviction as to the necessity for sympathy with and deep understanding of humanity is here set forth in the most admirably lucid and suggestive manner. Milton and Wordsworth are being compared:

You say, " I fear there is little chance of anything else in this life " — you seem by that to have been going through with a more painful and acute zest the same labyrinth that I have — I have come to the same conclusion thus far. My Branchings out therefrom have been numerous: one of them is the consideration of Wordsworth's genius and as a help, in the manner of gold being the meridian Line of worldly wealth, how he differs from Milton. And here I have nothing but surmises, from an uncertainty whether Milton's apparently less anxiety for Humanity proceeds from his seeing further or not than Wordsworth: and whether Wordsworth has in truth epic passion, and martyrs himself to the human heart, the main region of his song. . . .

I will return to Wordsworth — whether or no he has an extended vision or a circumscribed grandeur — whether he is an eagle in his nest or on the wing. And to be more explicit and to show you how tall I stand by the giant, I will put down a simile of human life as far as I now perceive it; that is, to the point to which I say we both have arrived at. Well — I compare human life to a large Mansion of many apartments, two of which I can only describe, the doors of the rest being as yet shut upon me. The first we step into we call the Infant, or Thoughtless Chamber, in which we remain as long as we do not think. We remain there a long while, and notwithstanding the doors of the second Chamber remain wide open, showing a bright appearance, we care not to hasten to it; but are at length imperceptibly impelled by the awakening of the thinking principle within us — We no sooner get into the Second Chamber, which I shall call the Chamber of Maiden-Thought, than we become intoxicated with the light and the atmosphere. We see nothing but pleasant wonders, and think of delaying there forever in delight. However among the effects this breathing is father of is that tremendous one of sharpening one's vision into the heart and nature of Man — of convincing one's nerves that the world is full of Misery and Heartbreak, Pain, Sickness, and oppression — whereby this Chamber of Maiden-Thought becomes gradually darkened, and at the same time, on all sides of it, many doors are set open — but all dark — all leading to dark passages. We see not the balance of good and evil; we are in a mist, *we* are now in that state, we feel the " Burden of the Mystery." To this point was Wordsworth come, as far as I can conceive, when he wrote " Tintern Abbey," and it seems to me that his genius is explorative of those dark Passages. Now if we live, and go on thinking, we too shall explore them. He is a genius and superior to us, in so far as he can, more than we, make discoveries and shed a light in them. Here I must think Wordsworth is deeper than Milton, though I think it has depended more upon the general and gregarious advance of intellect than individual greatness of Mind. From the Paradise Lost, and the other Works of Milton, I hope it is not too presuming, even between ourselves, to say, that his Philosophy, human and divine, may be tolerably understood by one not much advanced in years. In his time, Englishmen were just emancipated from a great superstition, and Men had got hold of certain points and resting-places in reasoning which were too newly born to be doubted, and too much opposed by the Mass of Europe not to be thought ethereal and authentically divine. — Who could gainsay his ideas on virtue, vice, and Chastity in Comus just at the time of the dismissal of Cod-pieces and a hundred other disgraces? Who would not rest satisfied with his hintings at good and evil in the Paradise Lost, when just free from the Inquisition and burning in Smithfield? The Reformation produced such immediate and great benefits, that Protestantism was considered under the immediate eye of heaven, and its own remaining dogmas and superstitions then, as it were, regenerated, constituted those resting places and seeming sure points of Reasoning — from that I have mentioned, Milton, whatever he may have thought in the sequel, appears to have been content with these by his writings. He did not think into the human heart as Wordsworth has done. Yet Milton, as a Philosopher, had sure as great powers as Wordsworth. What is then to be inferred? O many things. It proves that there is really a grand march of intellect, it proves that a mighty Providence subdues the mightiest minds to the service of the time being, whether it be in human Knowledge or Religion.

In this comparison of Milton with Wordsworth some striking principles for the judgment of genius and poetic creation are suggested. The sentences in regard to the gregarious march of the human intellect, and the work of Providence in subduing the mightiest minds to the service of the time are indeed significant. The first reveals the cheery optimism so characteristic of Keats — in spite of occasional gloomy outbursts — in regard to the world's advance towards perfection, a " march of the human intellect " indicating a sense of steady progression, just as in *Hyperion* the poet visions a world in evolution passing successively from stage to stage. The second recalls Taine, who, it will be remembered, insists that only a genius of a type harmonious with the temper of his time can rise above mediocrity; that the men of great genius have always been reflectors of the spirit of their respective ages. Taine I believe is thinking for the most part of the mere surface manifestations of life in poetry, such as an atmosphere of gloom or joyousness, of pessimism or optimism, disbelief or faith, and so forth, and goes no further except as these elements may be considered as indicative of the deepest life processes. The idea of environmental influence as suggested by Keats, however, is slightly different. For him the fundamental in poetic greatness is determined not so much by the spirit of the age, as by intellectual and imaginative insight — the ability to understand the permanent facts of human life, rather than to grasp temporary moral, theological, or political problems. Yet Keats would hold, I should say, that though the greatest poets should be prophets of a higher ideal order, they can never be much more than the interpreters of the highest life and thought of their day; at least they are bound and restricted according to the level of the common intellect and the pressing needs of their own time.

Most pertinent to the subject under direct discussion is the fact that we here find reiterated the idea that that poet is greatest who sees deepest into the secret of existence, and best portrays what he sees. Institutions, theology, matters of morality — all become proper subjects for high poetry in a limited sense only. And emphasis on any of them or all of them, with the eternal laws of human nature subordinated, leads to poetry in its nature inferior.

Interest in humanity and a capacity to martyr oneself to, and think into the human heart become, then, the median line of poetic greatness. It is true that the highest poetic power is to be measured by the ability to penetrate into the " dark passages " leading to the shrouded chamber of the " Mystery," [8] and " make discoveries and shed light on them "; but the necessary condition to an understanding of the " Burden of the Mystery " is that the vision " into the heart and nature of man " shall be sharpened, and that the nerves be convinced of the suffering and misery of the world. Moreover, this power is to be attained through a gradual evolutionary, educative process, in which the intellect expands from a thoughtless stage to one where all knowledge and wisdom

---

[8] He elsewhere calls it " the Penetralium of mystery." " Coleridge, for instance, would let go by a fine isolated veri-similitude caught from the Penetralium of mystery, from being incapable of remaining content with half knowledge."   Forman. Vol. IV, p. 50.

will be its province,[9] and all insight and understanding its highest goal.

All this seems to furnish unmistakable proof that Keats would make the human heart the main region of a poet's song and the world of reality the proper field for his endeavor. But we must not forget the obverse side of the shield, the legends of which have been displayed earlier in this chapter. The young poet could never for long escape his feeling for the poetic experience as one of detachment in an ideal dream-world existence, abstracted and separated from the visible and real; he was never able to suppress entirely his innate longing to fly away on " the viewless wings of Poesy," and in a realm of abstractions to forget " The weariness, the fever, and the fret " of actual life.

Sometimes, pendulum-like, swinging between the extremes, but more often earnestly endeavoring to find a means to a harmonious compromise, Keats's mind occupied itself with these sharply conflicting claims. How were they to be reconciled? The progress the poet made toward a reconciliation I shall show later. But before coming directly to that, it is necessary to examine closely-related phases of Keats's thought that have bearing on his more mature theories. The Mansion of Life letter marks a high water level in the young poet's emphasis on knowledge of humanity and insight into the " Mystery " as requisites to great poetry. It also furnishes the most concise expression of Keats's ideas as to the evolution of a poet's powers to a place where he may know and understand. In the next two chapters I shall trace the main lines of his thinking that led up to this point.

[9] Robert Bridges, in his introduction to the G. Thorn Drury Edition of Keats, p. xxxiii, points out the similarity in thought between Wordsworth's *Tintern Abbey, Sleep and Poetry,* and the Mansion of Life letter; Mr. de Selincourt in the Introduction to his edition of the poems, p. xxxix, comments upon the same likeness; so does Sidney Colvin in *John Keats,* pp. 127, 128, though he justly criticizes Mr. Bridges' choice of illustrative passages; Mary Suddard also briefly comments on the same point in her *Essays and Studies,* p. 38.

CHAPTER III

GRADUS AD PARNASSUM

KEATS has often been likened to the Greeks, and there were undoubtedly elements in him that suggest his kinship with the best representatives of the Hellenic spirit. He sought their reposeful serenity; he had their quick, warm imagination; he felt much of their naïve response to the sensuous beauty of the earth. But there was this vital difference: Keats was an Englishman, living in the nineteenth century. If the high poetic repose of the Attic sculptors seemed all desirable to him, it was much more difficult to attain. His was not the self-contained world of Phidias and Sophocles. Fate had placed Keats in an age when poetic thought was turning passionately toward an understanding of life and the universe, was insistently reaching out for a glimpse of the " unworldly blossom, the blue flower," that larger spirit palpitating behind all visible life and nature. And Keats very early, too, found himself instinctively seeking these same things. Unsatisfied with the narrow world of sight and sense, he threw himself into an earnest quest for a larger insight and understanding, eagerly striving to pierce the white shroud, for a vision of that higher unity that lies just beyond the ken of men.

But just as Plato had perceived that in the quest for absolute beauty, one cannot rise at one bound to complete apprehension, but the mind must pass from a view of particular things of beauty through ever widening circles, becoming first acquainted with the lesser objects preparatory to an understanding of the supreme ideal,[1] so Keats became early convinced that poetic power and poetic insight could not come at a single leap, but must rather evolve through successive

[1] *Symposium.* Section 211.

48

gradations in conformity with the poet's growing maturity and experience in his art and life.

In the Mansion of Life letter, quoted in the last chapter, we find this idea most admirably and succinctly stated. Here Keats conceives the intellect as expanding from a thoughtless stage to one where all knowledge and wisdom, hence all insight, will be its province. Possibly under the influence of Wordsworth, the poet suggests to us in this passage a rough parallel with the main lines of poetic development as set forth in *The Prelude;* and, as Robert Bridges, Sidney Colvin, and other critics have pointed out, there is also a close likeness between the stages in the different " chambers " and those outlined in *Tintern Abbey.*

As in *Tintern Abbey,* too, it is evident that with Keats the sensuous and the world of nature are chiefly significant in poetry as leading to an understanding of the deeper spirit of man and the " Mystery."

This becomes apparent in the 1817 volume of poems. It is true that in *I Stood Tip-Toe* and in the *Epistle to George,* in particular, nature seems to play an important part. But after all it is a subordinate part, the rôle of chief exciter of the imagination, and the poetry evoked by nature has all a human quality. Especially is this true in the evident warmth of sympathy in the passages relating to Pan and Syrinx, to Narcissus and Echo, and to Cynthia and Endymion in *I Stood Tip-Toe.* Nature in itself in this poem, which might well be entitled " The Influence of Nature on the Poet," is not suggested as a direct topic for poetry. But to nature the poet goes for inspiration. " Maker of sweet poets," Keats calls her —

> For what has made the sage or poet write
> But the fair paradise of Nature's light?
>
> (ll. 126–127.)

That this is true, as the succeeding lines show, is evidenced by the fact that in the very cadence and rhythm and tempo of poetry there is re-expressed what the poet saw or felt in

nature — its grandeur, its silences, its luxury. The poet then
goes on to point out this influence in greater detail:

> So felt he, who first told, how Psyche went
> On the smooth wind to realms of wonderment;
> What Psyche felt, and Love, when their full lips
> First touch'd.   (ll. 141–144.)

It is nature that furnishes the inspiration, the starting point,
for the fainter gleamings that shoot over the fancy:

> What first inspired a bard of old to sing
> Narcissus pining o'er the untainted spring?
> In some delicious ramble, he had found
> A little space, with boughs all woven round;
> And in the midst of all, a clearer pool
> Than e'er reflected in its pleasant cool,
> The blue sky here, and there, serenely peeping
> Through tendril wreaths fantastically creeping.
>   (ll. 164–171.)

And so the old poetry came to be. One glimpse through forest
boughs is enough to start to life visions of " Nymphs, Fauns,
and Satyrs," and an evening on a hilltop in the clear smiling
moonlight is sufficient to inspire the birth of the Endymion-
Cynthia romance.

Here Keats gives us in embryo his young theory of the
relation of nature to the artist and his work. In the presence
of natural objects of unusual beauty or significance, the poet
becomes oblivious of the present world. He loses himself in
contemplation, becomes detached from his surroundings, as
" fainter-gleamings " shoot over his fancy, and visions of
human form appear, until presently his imagination takes
wing, and poetic creation is accomplished. But as I have
said, even here this poetry is specifically of human quality,
though it is a humanity far removed from the actual world;
nature is the means not the end. In *Sleep and Poetry*, written
at about the same time as *I Stood Tip-Toe* and probably
finished somewhat earlier, the emphasis upon humanity is
unmistakable. The view expressed here is not inconsistent

with that of *I Stood Tip-Toe;* it is merely another aspect of
his thought that through nature the poet ascends to an understanding of man. Here, as in the Mansion of Life letter,
Keats had suggested a progression for himself in the unfolding
of his poetic life. Here, too, the sensuous seems to furnish
the stepping stone to the higher realms:

> First the realm I'll pass
> Of Flora, and Old Pan; sleep in the grass,
> Feed upon apples red, and strawberries,
> And choose each pleasure that my fancy sees.
>
> (ll. 101–104.)

This is the Thoughtless Chamber, the period of revelry in the
charms of nature and in mythological fancies bred by nature
— the sensuous period, as it were. But he cannot be content
here; he must pass on to a " nobler life," where he may find
the agonies and the strife of human hearts, the true end of
poetic endeavor.

A study of *Sleep and Poetry* and the Mansion of Life letter
shows with what healthy sanity Keats looked at the whole
matter of becoming a great poet. It is not strange that with
his lofty reverence for poetry he should see that the ascents
to the pinnacles of success were not to be easy. Only through
the mellowing influences of time, the ripening effects of trial
and failure, can a poet reach the point of penetration ìnto
the " Burden of the Mystery ":

> O for ten years, that I may overwhelm
> Myself in poesy; so I may do the deed
> That my own soul has to itself decreed.
>
> (*Sleep and Poetry*, ll. 96–98.)

Moreover, it is to be at the cost of tremendous effort, of the
severest kind, an agonizing, heart-breaking striving toward
the goal:

> . . . How much toil!
> How many days! What desperate turmoil!
> Ere I can have explored its widenesses.
>
> (ll. 307–309.)

The very notion that he may ever succeed seems almost pre-
sumptuous, but he has resolved, even though his young infirmities are painfully apparent. He has caught a vision of
what poetry should be; a "vast idea" rolls before him, and
no difficulties, however real and great, shall daunt him:

> What though I am not wealthy in the dower
> Of spanning wisdom; though I do not know
> The shiftings of the mighty winds that blow
> Hither and thither all the changing thoughts
> Of man: though no great minist'ring reason sorts
> Out the dark mysteries of human souls
> To clear conceiving: yet there ever rolls
> A vast idea before me, and I glean
> Therefrom my liberty; thence too I've seen
> The end and aim of Poesy.   (ll. 283–292.)

Nothing testifies more strongly to the sound critical judgment of Keats than that he thus early perceives that, though
he knows what is to be done, he cannot expect to realize his
ideals until he has passed through a period of arduous apprenticeship. His reach exceeds his grasp, and he is fully aware of
it; moreover, because he has reasoned the thing through, he
accepts the situation philosophically. "A vast idea" rolls
before him; he will follow it where it leads, even though as
yet no "great ministering reason" sorts out for him "the dark
mysteries of human souls," and the way, therefore, must be
long and hard. Meantime, he will advance as swiftly as may
be from "the region of Flora and old Pan," towards the
realms of higher conceiving, where he, too, may explore the
shaded chamber of the "Burden of the Mystery."

In *Endymion*, we find a further expression of Keats's conception of the route to the heights of great poetry, and of
the part nature and man must take in the upward climb.
When Keats wrote *Endymion*, his mind, he tells Shelley, was
"like a pack of scattered cards." He was, he admits, only
"straining at particles of light in the midst of a great darkness." Yet there is every reason to believe that in *Endymion*

we should find Keats's most mature thought up to that time. The poem was begun after a spring of three intense poetical experiences. Early in March or the last of February, Keats had been introduced to the Elgin Marbles. How profoundly they affected him we know from the two sonnets and the *Ode on a Grecian Urn* for which they undoubtedly furnished the inspiration. To Keats the study of the Elgin Marbles raised the whole range of vexing problems as to the relation between art and truth and beauty. But we shall come to that later.

Secondly, he was re-reading Shakespeare with eager intensity and complete delight. His April and May letters to Hunt, Haydon, and Reynolds show how he revelled in his master.

His third experience was something less than a month in solitude on the Isle of Wight. Along in April, 1817, Keats's brothers had decided that he needed a rest and a vacation. So they bundled him off to the Isle of Wight. Here he was much alone, and it appears that he employed much of his time in concentrated thought on poetry; for it was shortly after his return that he wrote to Leigh Hunt that at the Isle of Wight he had thought so much about poetry, so long together, that he could not get to sleep at night. " I was too much in solitude, and consequently was obliged to be in continual burning of thought," he declares.

Thus it was that with a newly stimulated mind and in burning thought on the problems of poetry *Endymion* was begun. It seems logical to find something of all this reflected in the substance of the poem.

I have noted in my first chapter, the various interpretations of *Endymion* that have been offered by different critics, all of them based upon allegory. There are those who decry any attempt to read allegorical meaning into the poem. Mr. George Saintsbury is one of these. In his contribution to the centenary volume, he voices his protest. He has been told, he says, that now, " You must busy yourself with its

problems; present the Latmian with a complete set of allegorical, symbolical, and all sorts of other *ical* explanations."
But as for himself, he has no patience with that sort of thing.
"Thank goodness," he exclaims, "no one ever suggested anything of that kind to me in the Boilers sixty-years since."
Another recent protest against an allegorical interpretation
has come from Amy Lowell in her notable biography of Keats.
"As to allegory," she declares, "that was completely foreign
to Keats's nature. There is no trace of allegory to be found
anywhere in his works." Symbolism she finds in *The Fall of
Hyperion,* and the *Endymion* "is full of suggestions," is, in
fact, "one of the most suggestive poems in English literature," but nowhere is there allegory.

Yet there are passages in the poem that seem to make allegorical interpretation inevitable. Keats himself invited just
this when, in revising his manuscript, he wrote to John Taylor,
his publisher, in January, 1818, altering and adding to the
passage beginning with "Wherein lies happiness?" in Book I,
the passage which above all others most plainly reveals allegory. I quote from the letter containing the amended
reading. It will be seen that the poet has added the lines
beginning with "In that which becks" and ending with "free
of space" — a significant addition indeed when considered in
connection, first, with its immediate context, and, then, with
the poem as a whole.

These lines as they now stand about "Happiness," have rung in
my ears like "a chime a mending." — See here,

> Behold
> Wherein lies happiness, Peona? fold, &c.

It appears to me the very contrary of blessed. I hope this will appear
to you more eligible.

> Wherein lies happiness? In that which becks
> Our ready minds to fellowship divine,
> A fellowship with Essence till we shine
> Full alchemized, and free of space — Behold
> The clear religion of Heaven — fold, &c.
>
> (*Endymion*, Book I, ll. 777-781.)

You must indulge me by putting this in, for setting aside the badness of the other, such a preface is necessary to the subject. The whole thing must, I think, have appeared to you, who are a consecutive man, as a thing almost of mere words, but I assure you that when I wrote it, it was a regular stepping of the Imagination towards a truth. My having written that argument will perhaps be of the greatest service to me of anything I ever did. It set before me the gradations of happiness, even like a kind of pleasure thermometer, and is my first step towards the chief attempt in the drama. The playing of different natures with joy and Sorrow.

Obviously, Keats understood himself to be saying more than appeared on the surface. This passage about " Happiness " was an " argument," that needed a preface to be understood. It was an argument, too, that was a revelation to himself, and was to be a first step " toward the chief attempt in the drama." When we recall, too, that this alteration was made upon mature reflection after the poem was completed,[2] and this section of it in the hands of the printers, it gains in importance. Not only, then, does this letter invite to a closer study of the inner significance of *Endymion,* but it suggests that in the " Wherein lies happiness " lines and the following should be found a clue to the real meaning of the poem.

Those who have interpreted *Endymion* as an allegory have been in agreement in making Endymion himself Man, Soul, or Poet in pursuit of an ideal. This seems inevitable. To me, Endymion is the poet in quest of the " Mystery," that is, of ultimate, ideal truth. I believe, too, that Keats was dimly outlining in this poem the successive stages of poetic development toward realization of this truth, and was, moreover, showing the relation of these gradations and experiences to each other. In other words, when in the final book it is disclosed that Cynthia, the ideal of sensuous beauty, the Indian Maiden, representative of the realities of earth, and the Moon, symbolic of the " Mystery," are one, Keats is declaring not only for the necessity of rising to a height of insight into the

---

[2] *Endymion* was finished in November, 1817. The following months Keats was copying the poem out for the press. See Colvin, *John Keats,* p. 162.

secret of the universe through the gradations of sensuous and human reality, but he is also asserting an essential final unity in the three orders — Nature, Humanity, and the higher spiritual essence. That is, a poet not only reaches an understanding of the ideal through deep and thorough intimacy, first, with the physical beauty of this world, then with the depths of human passion and suffering, but must find in the end that all merge into one.

The thought contained in this section on happiness bears out the idea of successive stages. Happiness — and Keats means the poet's goal — lies in that which invites our minds to " fellowship with essence." But this " fellowship divine " can be attained only through gradations " leading by degrees to the chief intensity." The first is a sort of higher sensuous stage, where the " airy stress of music's kiss " touches the free winds and unbinds the Aeolian magic. Old songs, old ditties, " ghosts of melodious prophesyings, rave." And at the instant of feeling all these things,

> . . . that moment have we stept
> Into a sort of oneness, and our state
> Is like a floating spirit's.
>
> (Book I, ll. 795–797.)

But there are richer entanglements than these sensuous ones, " enthralments far more self-destroying." The highest of these is love and friendship. Love is at the very " tip-top," " an orbed drop of light." Then follows an enlargement upon the luxuries of the passion of love, a love in which most men are content to live and " let occasion die." Beyond this human love is a love immortal.

> Now, if this earthly love has power to make
> Men's being mortal, immortal; to shake
> Ambition from their memories, and brim
> Their measure of content: what merest whim,
> Seems all this poor endeavor after fame,
> To one, who keeps within his steadfast aim
> A love immortal, an immortal too.
>
> (Book I, ll. 843–849.)

Mr. Fausset declares this merely "a rebellion against Keats's surrender to ravishment," but it appears rather a continuation of the main argument after a little side excursion into a region of pleasing aspect. In *Endymion* the poet could not resist such temptations to wander afield. "Must not lovers of poetry have a little region to wander in?" asks Keats in defending this same diffuseness in his verse. And we must grant that in this poem he gave sufficient space to satisfy the most ambitious, greedy rover. But underneath all is a substance of thought, none the less real because sometimes all but concealed. So here he means that he is ever keeping his eye steadfastly fixed on the final goal of poetry, an understanding of the Mystery, his "immortal love" (represented by the Moon), that above all mortal passion and all the treasures of all the sensuous world, is that loftiest realm of the super-sensuous world, into whose heights the true poet must ascend.

The allegory of *Endymion* seems to me to be this: In the first trance-like state on the hillside, when Endymion's enraptured gaze falls on the moon, the poet gets a glimpse of the ultimate goal for poetic endeavor, the Mystery. But the entrancingly beautiful heavenly maiden, with "blush-tinted cheeks," and a "paradise of lips and eyes," who then wafts herself down to him from the skies, is merely symbolic of sensuous beauty, the poet's first love.

I interpret the first whirling in the empyrean with the beautiful apparition as his first wild taste of sensuous beauty — the trance-like states, the stage of nymphs and knights and blisses. The second, in Book II, was a far deeper experience with sensuous reality; it was an illuminating, enriching experience, in which, after drinking to the depths the soul of the sensuous world, Endymion feels the first stirrings of the breath of human sympathy. It is nearly the same experience that Wordsworth describes in *Tintern Abbey,* when he says,

> For I have learned
> To look on nature, not as in the hour
> Of thoughtless youth; but hearing oftentimes

> The still sad music of humanity,
> Nor harsh nor grating, though of ample power
> To chasten and subdue.

Similar, but not identical, for with Keats it is not communion with nature alone, but with all sensuous objects, including the surface and seeming of humanity, that opens the way to the richer, more ennobling heights of sympathetic insight into the soul of man and the heart of all reality.

This second book represents the poetic soul under the full dominion of sensuous beauty. Those critics who have found in this part of the poem full proof of Keats's absorption in weak and amorous sentimentality should be reminded that the state of poetic development here symbolized is not Keats's ideal, but is a necessary step in the ascent toward the higher plane. This is, however, an advanced stage in the " Thoughtless Chamber "; it represents the " awakening of the thinking principle," and is even at the gradation where the poet's mind by insensible degrees advances into " the Chamber of Maiden-Thought." The first flush of delight in the physically luxurious has passed; here is communion with, a complete penetration into, the spirit of the sensuous.

The setting is in harmony with the idea of an apotheosis of the sensuous. The narrative movement takes Keats into the " sparry hollows of the world." It is a subterranean region of magnificent grandeur, of giant ranges of " sapphire columns," of fantastic bridges spanning crystal floods, of towering ocean cliffs shadowing the vast beneath, of diamond balustrades mounting beyond the reach of eye, and, finally, of exquisitely fashioned love chambers and " jasmine bowers bestrewn with golden moss." It is a world of sensuous delight, and Keats lets loose the reins of fancy in its building.

The two events of moment are the awakening of Adonis by Venus and the long impassioned love union with the heavenly apparition — Cynthia, in disguise, here representative of sensuous beauty. As described by the poet this is a scene of the most death-like intensity of sensual love. But let us remember that this is symbolic, and, regretful as the scene is, it loses some of its vulgarity. It is the only way Keats knows, just now, of representing the consummation of the marriage of the poetic soul with the spirit of sensuous beauty. And from that marriage has come new vision, new insight, new power, just as an understanding of the physical universe must always impart new vigor to the wings of thought:

> And now, thought he,
> How long must I remain in jeopardy
> Of blank amazements that amaze no more?
> Now I have tasted her sweet soul to the core
> All other depths are shallow; essences,
> Once spiritual,[3] are like muddy lees,
> Meant but to fertilize my earthly root,
> And make my branches lift a golden fruit
> Into the bloom of heaven.[4]
>
> (Book II, ll. 901–909.)

It is at this moment that we step

> Into a sort of oneness, and our state
> Is like a floating spirit's,

the moment described in the revelatory passage on "Happiness," of Book I. It is so deep a draught of sensuous beauty that it almost wafts the soul to higher airs, for now, after tasting "her sweet soul to the core," he feels stirring within him awakened sympathy for human beings. When he chances upon Arethusa and Alpheus in their woe — loving, but unable to realize their love because of Diana's wrath — he feels a glow of divine compassion:

> . . . he wept, and said: 'I urge
> Thee, gentle Goddess of my pilgrimage,
> By my eternal hopes, to soothe, to assuage,
> If thou art powerful, these lovers' pains;
> And make them happy in some happy plains.
>
> (Book II, ll. 1013–1016.)

---

[3] The first trance-like ecstasies in physical beauty.

[4] Note that growth to this new stature, which at the instant seems godlike, has come through progress from former stages of poetic experience.

So has the marriage with the soul of the sensuous world proved a stepping stone to a union with the spiritual beauty of human friendship and love.

The essential adventure in the third book is one in human friendship and sympathy. The scene is under the sea. I shall not stop to describe the

> . . . hollow vast, that foam'd
> Above, around, and at his feet;
>
> (Book III, ll. 120–121.)

with its bed of sands and pearls, its fretted roofs and its crystal palace, where lie rows and rows of lovers drowned in times gone by. It is enough to explain that here, coming upon old Glaucus, bound, under the spell of Circe, to paralyzed existence on the ocean bed, while his soul is torn by love for dead Scylla, Endymion's heart is touched, even as it was at sight of the sorrow of Alpheus and Arethusa, and he responds to the old man's pleas by aiding in his release and in the awakening of Scylla and all the thousands of lovers lying drowned in the crystal palace of the sea.

It is all an act of human love and sympathy that prepares the poet's spirit for the next higher experience, a complete union of the soul with the heart of humanity, which is the final key to the Penetralium of Mystery, the last step to the altar of high poetic insight, the lamp to illuminate "the passages all dark" leading to the "Burden of the Mystery."

For Endymion's relations with the Indian Lady in Book IV are not merely representative of the sensual love of man for woman. It is true there is some of that in it, too, as one of the highest human passions, yet it is not the love passion alone that is portrayed here, any more than is the love of Holiness for Una mere physical love, though it is represented as such. But the union with the Indian Maiden is the marriage of the soul of a poet with the spirit of sorrow and suffering in the world, with the "Misery and Heartbreak, Pain, Sickness, and Oppression" of mankind. The thing that impels

Endymion to a decision is not the mere loveliness of the Indian
Maiden; it is her desolation, her sad song of sorrow. For
even as the maiden sang in surrender,

> Come then, Sorrow!
> Sweetest Sorrow!
> Like an own babe I nurse thee on my breast:
> I thought to leave thee
> And deceive thee,
> But now of all the world I love thee best.
> (Book IV, ll. 279–284.)

so Keats believed that the poet must find in the tragedy of
the world his poetic salvation, that of all things of the universe,
he must cherish sorrow first. And it is directly to the poet
Keats is speaking, when the Indian Lady concludes:

> There is not one,
> No, no, not one,
> But thee to comfort a poor lonely maid;
> Thou art her mother,
> And her brother,
> Her playmate, and her wooer in the shade.
> (Book IV, ll. 285–290.)

Endymion's response is further corrobation of the fact that
this new alliance is with the world's sorrows:

> Poor lady, how thus long
> Have I been able to endure that voice?
> Fair Melody! kind Syren! I've no choice;
> I must be thy sad servant evermore:
> I cannot choose but kneel here and adore.
> (Book IV, ll. 288–293.)

It is true there is some attempt to carry out the episode as a
purely human love affair. But this does not go far. Hardly
has Endymion made his vow until the gods take a hand.
Mercury appears, swoops down to the earth, and is away.
From the turf outspring " two steeds jetblack." Upon these,
the lover and the lady soar away into space. They are carried
to the very bourne of Cynthia's realm and, in a dream, En-

dymion looks his vision — the Mystery — full in the face, at first without recognition; then, knowing her, he springs toward her, forgetful of " earth, and air and pains and care and suffering." In the act he awakes and finds the dream come true,[5] but by his side the beauteous Indian Lady still lies, and he is torn by conflicting desire for the immortal love and the earthly maid. But full realization cannot be yet. Cynthia fades away.

Back upon earth, in perplexity and in a mood of sorrowful renunciation Endymion is to discover that the Indian Lady is Cynthia herself, the Moon, in another form, even as had been the heavenly maiden in Books I and II. The heavenly dream maiden, or sensuous beauty, the Indian Lady, or humanity, and Cynthia the Moon, or ideal beauty, are all one.

So, first, through such close union with the spirit of the sensuous world that he catches from her, breathings of higher things beyond, and, second, through unconscious communion with the Mystery in the form of human passion and suffering, his sympathies with humanity having been enlarged to this capacity by means of contact with love and sorrow, the poet is able to envisage human passion completely, and in this he attains to union with his immortal love, the " Mystery." Thus, through nature and the sensuously beautiful in man, the poet learns to know the human heart, and through the human heart, the secret of all worth knowing in the universe. And in the end he finds united in one ideal the visions that drew him on in pursuit of each.

[5] " The Imagination," says Keats, " may be compared to Adam's dream; he awoke and found it truth." To Bailey. Nov., 1817. Forman. Vol. IV, p. 47.

CHAPTER IV

"SENSATION" VERSUS KNOWLEDGE
AND PHILOSOPHY

OF all English poets it may be safely said of Keats that he was by nature the most deeply sensitive. He felt with his whole being. His nervous organization was so delicately adjusted that the mere presence of very beautiful or ugly objects often threw him into violent extremes of sensation. As Lowell declares of him, " He could feel sorrow with his hands." It was possibly this fine susceptibility that led the young poet, as naturally as leaves come to a tree, to put his entire trust, in his early days, in intuitional, rather than in reasoned knowledge. He could well have cried with Whitman,

> Yet again, lo! the soul above all science.

For he felt that through the power of the imaginative activity the soul can know things that the reason can never understand. It is only the soul that can speak directly to the soul, only the soul that can ascend to the infinite and, mingling with essence, bring back the fine flower of truth.

It is apparent that the trance-like experiences described in the early poems — in *I Stood Tip-Toe* and *To My Brother George,* for instance, — to which I have referred in Chapter II, are purely the result of feeling, with no basis whatever in knowledge. The poet simply yields himself to an indefinable emotional ecstasy, in which he loses himself in " realms of wonderment." This is poetic vision. In *Endymion,* while it is true that there is emphasis on understanding human sorrow and suffering, and some suggestion of contact with it, yet the experiences of the chief personage are largely in the form of visions, and strongly point to the trance-like state as the only condition of poetic seeing.

But there is evidence that in the last months of 1817, though there has been no positive change of thought on this matter, the poet is troubled by vague misgivings and has spent unquiet hours on the subject. This is suggested by his well known letter to Bailey, written November 22, 1817, on the imagination. Keats's argument is intended as a triumphant vindication of the claims of the pure imagination as opposed to reason. But there are phrases in it that reveal a trace of wavering, and perhaps the very energy and vehemence with which he defends and explains his creed may be taken as an indication of his need of fortifying himself against doubts as to whether after all reason and philosophy have not a place in poetic apprehension. Mr. de Selincourt suggests that the letter was probably written in a controversial mood, and that even at the time it expressed only one side of the truth as Keats saw it. (Introduction to *The Poems*, p. xxxviii.) The passage is quoted at length in the chapter on the imagination, and I give here only the sentences that bear directly on the present discussion. The poet has been dwelling on the authenticity of the imagination as a revealer of truth, and declares,

> I have never yet been able to perceive how anything can be known for truth by consecutive reasoning — and yet it must be. Can it be that even the greatest Philosopher ever arrived at his Goal without putting aside numerous objections? However it may be, O for a life of Sensations rather than of Thoughts!

By "sensations" Keats here means feelings or intuitions, the pure activity of the imagination, as Ernest de Selincourt, and later Sidney Colvin have pointed out.[1] Mr. de Selincourt

[1] I quote Sidney Colvin's interpretation:
"... if only the reader will bear one thing well in mind: that when Keats in this and similar passages speaks of 'Sensations' as opposed to 'Thoughts' he does not limit the word to sensations of the body, of what intensity or exquisiteness soever or howsoever instantaneously transforming themselves from sensation into emotion: what he means are intuitions of the

declares the whole letter to be " a passionate exaltation of that part of Wordsworth's creed, with which Keats had, doubtless, most natural sympathy, the belief that we

> do well to trust,
> Imagination's light when reason's fails.

But Keats is going to much greater lengths than did Wordsworth, especially in *The Excursion,* where this declaration occurs. For long before 1814, Wordsworth had conceded to philosophy and reason a high place in a poet's equipment, and *The Excursion* itself is filled with passages extolling the knowledge to be gained through thought and books. It is only at the point where reason fails that the older poet would trust to imagination alone. Keats would find no sure place for reason whatever — yet, after all, " there must be," he admits, half doubtingly.

However, in the winter and spring of 1817–1818, there came a great intellectual crisis in the life of the young poet. Whether it was through direct association with Wordsworth in January and February of 1818 — Wordsworth was in London during the winter and was much in the Hunt-Haydon-Keats circle — or through a more intelligent re-reading of *The Excursion,* or through his recent study of Milton, as Mr. de Selincourt thinks, or merely through the rapid maturity of his own thinking powers, one can only guess, but, whatever the cause, the effects were decisive.

During this period, there occurred in Keats's correspondence and in some of his verse a new note indicative of what must have approached a revolution in his thinking. He is now for the first time, in contrast to his November declaration to Bailey, emphasizing the need for knowledge and philosophy for himself as a poet, and he practically resolves to put aside writing until he can better fit himself for the task. The first

---

mind and spirit as immediate as these, as thrillingly convincing and indisputable, as independent of all consecutive stages and formal processes of thinking: almost the same things, indeed, as in a later passage of the same letter he calls ' ethereal musings.' " *John Keats,* p. 155.

distinct annunciation of these new ideas comes in his *Lines Written on a Lock of Milton's Hair,* enclosed in a letter to Bailey, January 23. Here he declares:

> For many years my offerings must be hushed;
> . . . vain is now the burning and the strife,

for

> Pangs are in vain, until I grow high-rife
>   With old Philosophy,
> And mad with glimpses of futurity.

By April, he is writing to John Taylor:

> I was proposing to travel North this summer. There is but one thing to prevent me. — I know nothing — I have read nothing — and I mean to follow Solomon's directions, 'Get learning — get understanding.' I find earlier days are gone by — I find that I can have no enjoyment in the world but continual drinking of knowledge. I find there is no worthy pursuit but the idea of doing some good in the world. Some do it with their society — some with their wit — some with their benevolence — some with a sort of power of conferring pleasure and good humour on all they meet — and in a thousand ways, all dutiful to the command of great Nature — there is but one way for me. The road lies through application, study, and thought. I will pursue it; and for that end purpose retiring for some years. I have been hovering for some time between an exquisite sense of the luxurious, and a love for philosophy, — were I calculated for the former, I should be glad. But as I am not, I shall turn all my soul to the latter.

It was at this time, too, he resolved to travel and see the world — first England, and Scotland, then all Europe. To that end, he planned the summer walking trip with Brown. Of his determination to garner, at first hand, the experience he was convinced he needed, he wrote to Haydon:

> I purpose within a month to put my knapsack at my back and make a pedestrian tour through the North of England, and part of Scotland — to make a sort of Prologue to the life I intend to pursue — that is to write, to study, and to see all Europe at the lowest expense. I will clamber through the Clouds and exist. I will get such an accumulation of stupendous recollections that as I walk through the suburbs of London I may not see them — I will stand upon Mount

Blanc and remember this coming Summer when I intend to straddle
Ben-Lomond — with my soul! — galligaskins are out of the Question.

It is significant that it was during this period that the
Mansion of Life letter, quoted in my second chapter, was
written. One will recall the emphasis there upon philosophy
and wisdom as a basis for great poetry. In this same letter
Keats declares, " An extensive knowledge is necessary to
thinking people — it takes away the heat and fever; and
helps, by widening speculation, to ease the ' Burden of the
Mystery.' " Here too, he wrote, continuing his discussion of
Wordsworth:

> In regard to his genius alone — we find what he says true as far as
> we have experienced, and we can judge no further but by larger ex-
> perience — for axioms in philosophy are not axioms till they are
> proved upon our pulses. We read fine things, but never feel them to
> the full until we have gone the same steps as the author. — I know
> this is not plain; you will know exactly my meaning when I say that
> now I shall relish Hamlet more than I have ever done — Or better —
> You are sensible no man can set down Venery as a bestial or joyless
> thing until he is sick of it, and therefore all philosophizing on it would
> be mere wording. Until we are sick, we understand not; in fine, as
> Byron says, " Knowledge is sorrow "; and I go on to say that " Sorrow
> is wisdom " — and further for aught we can know for certainty " Wis-
> dom is folly."

From all this it would appear that the swing from the earlier
theory of pure sensation is complete. Keats's emphasis upon
wisdom and philosophy to be gained through study, thought,
and first-hand experience is unmistakable. In fact, at first
glance one might think that the life of the imagination is to
be abandoned altogether. But Keats has no thought of that.
He has simply found that philosophy and reason have a place
in poetry, and that, so far from being antagonistic to the
imagination, they are really adjuncts to it, and furnish the
only true and proper basis for its development to the highest
possible reaches. Only through study and experience can the
mind be so strengthened that the imagination shall have a

substance to it adequate to the production of great poetry. A
further study of extracts from Keats's writings of the time
makes this clear. In the same Mansion of Life letter, from
which I have so frequently quoted, a letter so rich in significant passages that it might well be taken as a test for
Keats's whole aesthetic thought of this period, he declares,

> Were I to study Physic or rather Medicine again, I feel it would not
> make the least difference in my Poetry. . . . Every department of
> Knowledge we see excellent and calculated toward a great whole.[2] I
> am so convinced of this that I am glad at not having given away my
> medical Books, which I shall again look over to keep alive the little I
> know thitherwards. . . .

And to Bailey he wrote,

> I should not have consented to myself these four months tramping
> in the highlands, but that I thought it would give me more experience,
> rub off more prejudice, use me to more hardship, identify finer scenes,
> load me with grander mountains, and strengthen more my reach in
> Poetry, than would stopping at home among books, even though I
> should reach Homer.

It is plain that both knowledge and experience are to be
sought for the sake of poetic power. All this load of experiences has for its objective the preparation of a poet for his
great task. Keats had evidently become dissatisfied with
poetry that had no firm basis in the world of thought and
reality, an idea he expressed vigorously to Haydon nearly a
year later in these words:

> I am convinced of this, and from this I have come to this resolu-
> tion — never to write for the sake of writing or making a poem, but
> from running over with any little knowledge or experience which many
> years of reflection may perhaps give me; otherwise I will be dumb.

Mere sensation will no longer do. Poetry must be based
on something more certain than mere feeling, or intuition, by

---

[2] " The poet, described in ideal perfection, brings the whole soul of man
into activity, with the subordination of its faculties to each other according
to their relative dignity and worth."

Coleridge: Biographia Literaria.

itself. Keats was at this time in a state where his whole being demanded certainties; he was planning to taste life to the full that he might garner a rich sheaf of personal experiences to serve as authentic background for imaginative creation later. In January, he had written to his brothers, " Nothing is finer for the purposes of great production than a very gradual ripening of the intellectual powers." And then he had gone on by way of illustration to quote his sonnet *On sitting down to read King Lear once again*." In this sonnet are lines that show the particular bearing Keats felt that a " gradual ripening of the intellectual powers " and a load of rich experiences might have on great production:

> Chief Poet! and ye clouds of Albion,
>   Begetters of our deep eternal theme,
> When through the old oak forest I am gone,
>   Let me not wander in a barren dream,
> But when I am consumed in the fire,
>   Give me new Phoenix wings to fly at my desire.

"Let me not wander in a barren dream," Keats is praying to his great master, " but when I take flights into the dream-world, give me the new wings of an imagination full-fledged in knowledge of the world and experience." As Mr. de Selincourt declares, in his Warton Lecture on Keats:

The significance of this appeal to Shakespeare is clear enough. As he faces, in *King Lear,* a pitiless reality, he sees that he has unwittingly belittled even that golden-tongued romance which has first awakened his poetic life, but which now he lays aside. For " in the old oak forest " our dreams need not be barren: Spenser's poetic world, for instance, was far away, but he took there a mind and a heart stored with memories of his own experience. Keats realizes that if he too is to be a " man of achievement," he must learn to think and feel.

Keats had found that flights of the imagination into the dream-world with wings unladen with the fertilizing pollen of the wisdom of human knowledge were unfruitful. The poetic world itself is a world of abstractions; but, unless the poet

carries with him in dream-flight a soul made wise by contact
with nature and humanity, a memory loaded with rich human experiences and adventure into the heights and depths of
life, that flight will be a barren one, and will end in empty,
aimless soaring.   For Keats's best statement of this idea we
must turn again to the admirable Mansion of Life letter:

> The difference of Sensations with and without knowledge appears to
> me this: in the latter case we are falling continually ten thousand
> fathoms deep and being blown up again, without wings, and with all
> the horror of a bare-shouldered creature — in the former case, our
> shoulders are fledged, and we go through the same air and space
> without fear.

Thus Keats picturesquely summarizes the whole truth of
the matter, as he had arrived at it by the May of 1818.   So
now he demands knowledge.   It is not that a poet should give
up the life of Sensations entirely, though it is true that in a
few extreme moments he seems to suggest that; it is merely
that when excursions into the world of abstractions are taken,
the shoulders should be full-fledged, the flight on the wings
of an educated, disciplined imagination, rather than on the
bare sails of fruitless fancy.   In other words, there must be an
intellectual as well as an imaginative basis for poetry.

These early months of hard thinking in the winter and
spring of 1818 had indeed been fruitful.   Keats had suddenly
discovered a serious deficiency in his poetic equipment.   True
poetry required intellectual, philosophic, experiential background.   In these things, compared with great cosmopolitans
like Wordsworth and Milton, he found himself to be sadly
defective.   With unusual vigor and resolution, he determined
to remedy his lack.   His whole mind was for the time turned
in this direction.   It is not strange then that we should sometimes find him during this period stating the case for knowledge and wisdom with overemphasis — an overemphasis that
has led some critics to the conclusion that Keats had permitted his zeal for philosophy to override his belief in the
imaginative and poetic.   A study of all his utterances, how-

ever, proves that this was not the case: not only do the claims of the imagination continually present themselves, but they at times assert their rights so clamorously as seriously to threaten to dispossess philosophy entirely. All of which shows that though Keats had been able to state admirably the right relationship between sensation and philosophy, he had not yet been able to accept his reasoned conclusions; he could not yet see just how the marriage between the two faculties could be consummated. In a later chapter, I shall show how Keats gradually came to understand the means by which a poet could still adhere to his dream world and yet " envisage all reality " there, and how in so doing he arrived nearer the state toward which he aspired — " with the yearning Passion I have for the beautiful connected and made one with the ambition of my intellect."

CHAPTER V

THE "MYSTERY"

Read me a lesson, Muse, and speak it loud
    Upon the top of Nevis, blind in mist!
I look into the chasms, and a shroud
    Vapourous doth hide them, — just so much I wist
Mankind do know of hell; I look o'erhead,
    And there is sullen mist, — even so much
Mankind can tell of heaven; mist is spread
    Before the earth, beneath me, — even such,
Even so vague is man's sight of himself!
    Here are the craggy stones beneath my feet, —
Thus much I know that, a poor witless elf,
    I tread on them, — that all my eye doth meet
Is mist and crag, not only on this height,
But in the world of thought and mental might! [1]

In these lines, written under the brooding influence of mountain scenery, we find the poet restating in his own admirable way the old, old enigma of the ages: The universe and man! Why? What? Whither? By the time this poem was written this had become to Keats an urgent problem insistently demanding solution. Three weeks earlier, on the same walking trip with Brown during which he had seen Ben Nevis, he had come unexpectedly one morning in full view of Ailsa Rock, rising sheer, one thousand feet, out of the sea. Keats, it seems, surveyed the scene in awe and breathless wonder; it was sublime: Ailsa rearing her head high in misty vastness — it was raining — gave him a " complete idea of a deluge." " It was fifteen miles distant and seemed close upon us," he wrote to his brother Tom. . . . " Ailsa struck me very suddenly — really, I was a bit alarmed." Some of the mystery and sub-

---

[1] Written upon Ben Nevis, August 2, 1818. It was a cloudy, misty day, but at times the mist lifted leaving all clear. The poem was evidently composed at a time when the vapor had settled down thickly.

limity of it he put into a sonnet — the sonnet known as *To Ailsa Rock*. "When," asks the poet, as if fascinated and awed by a sense of the infinitude of old slow-moving time and of the magnitude of the power that underlies nature's long unfathomable processes,

> When were thy shoulders mantled in huge streams?
> When, from the sun, was thy broad forehead hid?
> How long is't since the mighty power bid
> Thee heave to airy sleep from fathoms dreams —

But Ailsa does not answer —

> Thou answer'st not; for thou art dead asleep;
> Thy life is but two dead eternities,
> The last in air; the former in the deep!

Again the age-old query; again the failure to find a fit reply.

In these two sonnets there is expressed something of the "Burden of the Mystery" that throughout Keats's life so often weighed heavily upon his spirit. The Ben Nevis lines especially suggest a moment of agnosticism, and we detect in them a note that recalls old Omar's sad confession of the futility of thought:

> Earth could not answer, nor the Seas that mourn
> In flowing Purple, of their Lord forlorn.

For it seems that Keats, like Omar, was facing here a "Door to which" he "found no Key," a "Veil through which" he "could not see." But this is only a temporary mood; he still strives hopefully to pierce the veil. As we have seen, it becomes a part of his poetic creed that the mystery must be solved, and he finds no rest nor peace of mind until the burden upon his mind is lightened. Some of his attempts to unravel the tangled skein amply demonstrate with what near approach to prophetic vision the young poet had been endowed.

In considering this aspect of Keats's thought I wish to speak first of the more immediate phase of the Mystery which gave him unquiet hours, that is, the why of the pain and cruelty here on earth.

Contrary to the opinion so often held by critics, Keats approached life with vivid interest and wide-open eyes. He was not blind to the truth of Nature, as was Shelley, who perceived only beauty and harmony there; he saw her as she was, with all her cruel disregard of life, and anticipated by many years Tennyson's vision of " Nature, red in tooth and claw," shrieking " with ravine " against God's creed of love. Moreover, he felt with all the shock of which keen sensibility is capable the suffering of humanity.

The Epistle to Reynolds is a bit of verse remarkable as a commentary on Keats's reaction to these things. The epistle as a whole is really a running over in another form of that chain of thought that had been haunting his mind since he wrote *Sleep and Poetry* and was finally so adequately expressed in the Mansion of Life letter — the progressive steps in poetic development from the stage of the " Thoughtless Chamber " to that of a perception of the " Burden of the Mystery." But the latter part of the poem, as Mr. Bradley has clearly pointed out in his *Keats and " Philosophy,"* specifically reveals what aspect of things " most especially and constantly reminded Keats of ' the burden of the mystery.' " It shows, too, how heavily these things bore upon his spirit at this time.

> O that our dreamings all, of sleep or wake,
> Would all their colours from the sunset take:
> From something of material sublime,
> Rather than shadow our own soul's day-time
> In the dark void of night. For in the world
> We jostle, — but my flag is not unfurl'd
> On the Admiral-staff, — and so philosophize
> I dare not yet! Oh, never will the prize,
> High reason, and the love of good and ill,
> Be my award! Things cannot to the will
> Be settled, but they tease us out of thought;
> Or is it that imagination brought
> Beyond its proper bound, yet still confin'd,
> Lost in a sort of Purgatory blind,

Cannot refer to any standard law
Of either earth or heaven? It is a flaw
In happiness, to see beyond our bourn, —
It forces us in summer skies to mourn,
It spoils the singing of the Nightingale.

And then he comes to the specific starting point of all this mournful reflection:

Dear Reynolds! I have a mysterious tale,
And cannot speak it: the first page I read
Upon a Lampit rock of green sea-weed
Among the breakers; 'twas a quiet eve,
The rocks were silent, the wide sea did weave
An untumultuous fringe of silver foam
Along the flat brown sand; I was at home
And should have been most happy, — but I saw
Too far into the sea, where every maw
The greater on the less feeds evermore. —
But I saw too distinct into the core
Of an eternal fierce destruction,
And so from happiness I far was gone.

This relentless cruelty seems too awful to be borne; it sickens him, and he cannot banish the sight from his mental eye:

Still do I that most fierce destruction see, —
The Shark at savage prey, — the Hawk at pounce, —
The gentle Robin, like a Pard or Ounce,
Ravening a worm, . . .

How heavy sits the " Burden of the Mystery " upon the young shoulders of the poet! How glad would be a full escape from all such thoughts! But Keats knows full well that for him there is no escape. A month later almost to a day, April 25, he is writing, " There is but one way for me. The road lies through application, study, and thought. I will pursue it. . . . I have been hovering for some time between an exquisite sense of the luxurious, and a love for philosophy; were I calculated for the former, I should be glad. But as I am not, I shall turn all my soul to the latter."

Keats's attitude toward the whole vexing question of the

why of a cruel world is further shown by his reactions to human suffering. The sight and thought of physical misery among men and women filled the young poet with sorrow. In the presence of sickness and pain, he seems to have been moved to the point of feverish concern and pity. From his childhood, Keats had been in the midst of illness, suffering, and death. It must have been in a sad mood, pondering on these things, that he wrote to Fanny Brawne in July, 1819, " I have never known any unalloy'd Happiness for many days together: the death or sickness of some one has always spoilt my hours." When he was only nine years old, just after he had been put to school at Enfield, in 1804, his father was killed, his skull fractured by a fall from his horse. Six years later, in 1810, the mother died of consumption after a lingering illness, during which the affectionate lad John, facing the possibility of losing his second parent, hung over her with the most beautiful and patient devotion to the last. Then came the slow wasting away and death of the loved brother Tom, with Keats at his side always, watching, often in feverish agony, the certain dissolution of body going on before him. Something of this experience must be reflected in that line in the *Ode to a Nightingale*, when Keats is describing a world of fret and weariness and fever,

> Where youth grows pale and spectre-thin and dies.

How powerfully the whole situation affected him may be discerned from passages in his letters at this time. Passionately he wrote to Dilke: " I wish I could say Tom was any better. His identity presses upon me so all day that I am obliged to go out — and although I intended to have given some time to study alone, I am obliged to write and plunge into abstract images to ease myself of his countenance, his voice, and feebleness — so that I live now in a continual fever." One of the records we have of the effect of all this upon his thinking is that he was faced squarely by the problem of immortality. " I will not enter into any parsonic comments on death — yet the common observations of the commonest people on death are true as their proverbs. I have scarce a doubt of immortality of some nature or other — neither had Tom."

And we must not neglect another element in Keats's experience that brought him face to face with the mystery of pain and death. Keats served his term as a surgeon's apprentice, and must have seen at first hand some of the misery that sickness and disease bring. Before the days of improved methods and twilight sleep the practice of obstetrics furnished experiences that would move a heart of stone, while the crude surgery of the time, unalleviated by the blessing of anaesthetics, must have been a recurrent agony to a witness of Keats's sensitive nature. That the sufferings with which he came in contact here did not pass unrecorded in his impressionable brain is proved by later outbursts in his letters. To Benjamin Bailey, he declares:

One saying of yours I shall never forget — you may not recollect it — it being perhaps said when you were looking on the Surface and seeming of Humanity alone, without a thought of the past or the future — or the deeps of good and evil — merely you said, "Why should woman suffer?" Aye, why should she? "By heavens, I'd coin my very soul and drop my Blood for Drachmas." These things are, and he who feels how incompetent the most skyey Knight-errantry is to heal this bruised fairness, is like a sensitive leaf on the hot hand of thought.

Quite as significant is another passionate declaration to Bailey: "Were it my choice, I would reject a Petrarchal coronation — on account of my dying day,[2] and because women have cancers."

The mystery of human life and its evils were preying heavily on the spirit of Keats these days. In the beginning of the letter in which he cries out so sharply, "Why should woman

[2] In his article in the *John Keats Memorial Volume*, Professor Bradley interprets this as a vehement expression against death as an obvious evil, similar to, though more violent than, his usual attitude toward death in the letters as distinguished from his prevailing attitude in the poems — where he regards death as a "pure good, a friend, almost a Saviour." (P. 53, 54.) But a few lines farther down in this same letter we find,

suffer?" he has been saying, "Twelve days have pass'd since your last reached me. — What has gone through the myriads of human minds since the 12th? We talk of the immense Number of Books, the Volumes ranged thousands by thousands — but perhaps more goes through the human intelligence in Twelve days than ever was written. — *How has that unfortunate family lived through the twelve?*"

As Professor Bradley suggests in his *Keats and "Philosophy"* the results of all this musing on the "unfortunate family" of human beings is a more or less "settled conviction that wisdom is sorrow, happiness only to the thoughtless, life something to be 'undergone.'" Mr. Bradley says a "settled conviction" but I say "more or less settled," for Keats was not at all content to let the matter rest there. It is a fact that, writing from Scotland, after a visit to the Burns memorials, Keats could say, "It is true that out of suffering there is no dignity, no greatness, that in the most abstracted pleasure there is no happiness." But it is also a fact that in spite of his frequent revolt against the whole idea of dwelling on such matters, as, over and over, his abstraction-loving impulses asserted themselves, he was constantly, earnestly striving to find a solution to the "Mystery"; and perhaps in this solution he hoped to be able to discover a more smiling aspect of existence.

There are various passages in his letters wherein we see his mind at work reaching out after explanations. In November, 1817, he is venturing an opinion on the life after death. A life of "Sensations," he says, is "a shadow of reality to come — and this consideration has further convinced me, — for it has come as auxiliary to another favorite speculation of mine, — that we shall enjoy ourselves hereafter by having what we

---

"... and now I am never alone without rejoicing that there is such a thing as death — without placing my ultimate in the glory of dying for a great human purpose." Is not Keats rather saying then that he would reject a Petrarchal Coronation because in comparison with the glory of dying for a great human purpose such an empty honor would be insignificant? A close reading of the lines seems to show this to be his meaning.

called happiness on Earth repeated in a finer tone." And, again, a year later, in the same letter that contains the expression of his own and his brother Tom's conviction that there is some kind of immortality, he throws out a further suggestion as to the nature of the future life:

The goings on of the world makes me dizzy. There you are with Birkbeck — here I am with Brown — sometimes I fancy an immense separation, and sometimes as at present, a direct communication of Spirit with you. That will be one of the grandeurs of immortality. There will be no space, and consequently the only commerce between spirits will be by their intelligence of each other — when they will completely understand each other, while we in this world merely comprehend each other in different degrees — the higher the degree of good so higher is our Love and Friendship. I have been so little used to writing lately that I am afraid you will not smoke my meaning, so I will give you an example. Suppose Brown or Haslam or anyone whom I understand in the next degree to what I do you, were in America, they would be so much the farther from me in proportion as their identity was less impressed upon me. Now the reason why I do not feel at the present moment so far from you is that I remember your Ways and Manners and actions; I know your manner of thinking, your manner of feeling; I know what shape your joy or your sorrow would take; I know the manner of your walking, standing, sauntering, sitting down, laughing, punning, and every action so truly that you seem near to me. You will remember me in the same manner — and the more when I tell you I shall read a passage of Shakespeare every Sunday at ten o'clock — you read one at the same time, and we shall be as near each other as blind bodies can be in the same room.[3]

Here, in addition to some lively intimations of the nature of the human spirit in its possible power of annihilating space so that even in this world, under right conditions, there may be free "commerce" between sympathetic minds, no matter how distant from each other physically, Keats seems to be speaking as if upon at least one riddle of life, the question as to whether this world of pains is the be-all and the end-all, he has reached some fairly definite conclusions. There is to

[3] To George and Georgiana Keats. Dec., 1818. Forman. Vol. IV, p. 191.

be a future life of some kind; it is to be a pleasurable existence in which the happiness of earth is to be " repeated in a
finer tone "; in a universal understanding by its participants,
through direct spiritual communication, it is to have a grandeur all its own. But this does not in any sense mean that
Keats accepted the Christian religion. Keats admired Jesus,
and classed him with Socrates as one of the two entirely disinterested men who have lived on earth.[4] But he felt it was
to be lamented that the history of Jesus " was written and
revised by Men interested in the pious frauds of Religion."
Like Nietszche, Keats must have believed that there has lived
" only one Christian, and he died on the Cross." Perhaps on
his death-bed, he learned to believe that there had been born
a second, for Severn's beautiful disinterested care for him must
have seemed inspired by the Christ's teachings.

Though there is nothing in the poet's own writings to show
his trend that way, Severn records that in his last days Keats
became a Christian. Here is Mr. Severn's own account of it,
as it occurs in *The Vicissitudes of Keats's Fame,* published in
the *Atlantic Monthly,* April, 1863:

> On finding me inflexible in my purpose of remaining with him he
> became calm and tranquilly said that he was sure why I held up so
> patiently was owing to my Christian faith, — that he now felt con-
> vinced how much every human being required the support of religion
> that he might die decently. . . . "Now, my dear Severn, I am sure
> if you could get some of the works of Jeremy Taylor to read to me,
> I might become *really* a Christian, and leave this world in peace."
> . . . I read some passages to him, and prayed with him, and I could
> tell by the grasp of his dear hand that his mind was reviving. . . . At
> last I had the consolation of finding him calm, trusting, and more pre-
> pared for his end than I was. . . . In all he then uttered he breathed
> a simple Christian spirit; indeed, I always think that he died a
> Christian, that " Mercy " was trembling on his dying lips, and that
> his tortured soul was received by those Blessed Hands which could
> alone welcome it.

The most mature and complete expression of Keats's thinking on the whole vexing problem of life and its contradictions

4 See Chapter VI, p. 98.

is to be found in the long journal letter of the spring of 1819 written to his brother and sister-in-law in America. "Here," as Mr. Bradley explains, "he sets aside both the 'vale of tears' doctrine of popular orthodoxy and the 'perfectibility' doctrine of Dilke and Shelley, and, very apologetically, develops the idea that the obstacles and hardships which may seem mere lamentable evils, and to him had once seemed incompatible with the Beauty which yet must be truth, are necessary to the formation and development of individual souls." Keats in effect outlines a scheme of individual salvation, with the world not a "vale of tears," but a "vale of Soul-making"; the world is a school, and the human heart the "horn-book" of the school. He also suggests certain philosophical problems as to the nature and origin of life and the character of the ultimate reality. I know of nothing in all Keats's writings that carries the mind further in so many different directions, nothing that points more strongly to his mental struggles to understand the meanings and relationships of life's baffling phenomena, his persistent reaching out after truth in the light of his own experience and observation, nothing that shows how far he had gone toward a satisfactory philosophic reconciliation of the facts of existence. I quote the passage at length:

I have been reading lately two very different books, Robertson's America and Voltaire's Siècle de Louis XIV. It is like walking arm in arm between Pizarro and the great-little Monarch. In how lamentable a case do we see the great body of people in both instances; in the first when Men might seem to inherit quiet of Mind from unsophisticated senses; from uncontamination of civilization and especially from their being as it were estranged from the mutual helps of Society and its mutual injuries — and thereby more immediately under the Protection of Providence — even there they had mortal pains to bear as bad, or even worse than Bailiffs, Debts and Poverties of civilized Life. The whole appears to resolve into this — that Man is originally a poor forked creature subject to the same mischances as the beasts of the forest, destined to hardships and disquietude of some kind or other. If he improves by degrees his bodily accommodations and comforts — at each stage, at each ascent there are waiting for him a fresh set of annoyances — he is mortal and there is still a heaven with its Stars above his head. The most interesting question that can come before us is, How far by the persevering endeavors of a seldom appearing Socrates Mankind may be made happy — I can imagine such happiness carried to an extreme — but what must it end in? — Death — and who could in any such a case bear with death? The whole troubles of life which are now frittered away in a series of years, would then be accumulated for the last days of a being who instead of hailing its approach would leave this world as Eve left Paradise. But in truth I do not at all believe in this sort of perfectibility — the nature of the world will not admit of it — the inhabitants of the world will correspond to itself. Let the fish Philosophise the ice away from the Rivers in winter time and they shall be in continual play in the tepid delight of summer. Look at the Poles and at the Sands of Africa, whirlpools and volcanoes. Let men exterminate them and I will say that they may arrive at earthly Happiness. The point at which Man may arrive is as far as the parallel state in inanimate nature and no further. For instance suppose a rose to have sensation, it blooms on a beautiful morning, it enjoys itself, but then comes a cold wind, a hot sun — it cannot escape it, it cannot destroy its annoyances — they are as native to the world as itself — not more can man be happy in spite, the worldly elements will prey upon his nature. The common cognomen of this world among the misguided and superstitious is " a vale of tears " from which we are to be redeemed by a certain arbitrary interposition of God and taken to Heaven. What a little circumscribed straightened notion!

The Vale of Soul-Making

Call the world if you please " The vale of Soul-making." Then you will find out the use of the world. (I am speaking now in the highest terms for human nature admitting it to be immortal which I will here take for granted for the purpose of showing a thought which has struck me concerning it.) I say " Soul-making " — Soul as distinguished from an Intelligence. There may be intelligences or sparks of divinity in millions — but they are not Souls till they acquire identities, till each one is personally itself. Intelligences are atoms of perception — they know and they see and they are pure, in short they are God. — How then are Souls to be made? [5] How then are these

[5] There is a possibility that Hunt and Keats had talked on this subject of soul-making. At any rate it is worth noting the similarity of Hunt's ideas expressed in a letter to Shelley on the death of his child, William:

sparks which are God to have identity given them — so as ever to possess a bliss peculiar to each one's individual existence? How but by
the medium of a world like this? This point I sincerely wish to consider because I think it a grander system of salvation than the christian
religion — or rather it is a system of Spirit creation. This is effected
by three grand materials acting the one upon the other for a series
of years. These three materials are the *Intelligence* — the *human
heart* (as distinguished from intelligence or Mind), and the *World* or
Elemental space suited for the proper action of *Mind and Heart* on
each other for the purpose of forming the *Soul* or *Intelligence destined
to possess the sense of Identity*. I can scarcely express what I but
dimly perceive — and yet I think I perceive it — that you may judge
the more clearly I will put it in the most homely form possible. I
will call the *world* a School instituted for the purpose of teaching little
children to read — I will call the *human heart* the *horn Book* read in
that School — and I will call the *Child able to read, the Soul* made
from that School and its *horn book*. Do you not see how necessary a
World of Pains and troubles is to school an Intelligence and make it
a Soul? A Place where the heart must feel and suffer in a thousand
diverse ways. Not merely is the Heart a Hornbook, it is the Mind's
Bible, it is the Mind's experience, it is the text from which the Mind
or Intelligence sucks its identity.[6] As various as the Lives of Men
are — so various become their Souls, and thus does God make individual beings, Souls, Identical Souls of the sparks of his own essence.
This appears to me a faint sketch of a system of Salvation which does
not offend our reason and humanity — I am convinced that many difficulties which christians labour under would vanish before it — there
is one which even now strikes me — the salvation of Children. In

---

"I do not know that a soul is born with us; but we seem to me, to *attain*
to a soul, some later, some earlier; and when we have got that, there is a
look in our eye, a sympathy in our cheerfulness, and a yearning and grave
beauty in our thoughtfulness that seems to say, 'Our mortal dress may fall
off when it will; our trunk and our leaves may go; we have shot up our
blossom into an immortal air.'"

Hunt's *Correspondence*. Vol. I, p. 130.

[6] This idea as to the value of difficulties in the making of a man is not
a new one; back in May, 1817, he had written to Haydon:
"However, I must think that difficulties nerve the Spirit of a Man —
they make our Prime Objects a Refuge as well as a Passion. The Trumpet
of Fame is as a tower of Strength, the ambitious bloweth it and is safe."

Forman. Vol. IV, p. 18.

Let us add this comment from Dostioevsky:
"May it not be that man occasionally loves something besides prosperity? May it not be that he loves *adversity*? And may not adversity be
as good for him as happiness?" — *The Underworld*.

them the spark or intelligence returns to God without any identity —
it having had no time to learn of and be altered by the heart — or seat
of the human Passions. It is pretty generally suspected that the
christian scheme has been copied from the ancient Persian and Greek
Philosophers.[7] Why may they not have made this simple thing even
more simple for common apprehension by introducing Mediators and
Personages in the same manner as in the heathen mythology abstractions are personified? Seriously I think it probable that this system
of Soul-making may have been the Parent of all the more palpable and
personal schemes of Redemption among the Zoroastrians, the Christians and the Hindoos. For as one part of the human species must
have their carved Jupiter; so another part must have the palpable and
named Mediator and Saviour, their Christ, their Oromanes and their
Vishnu. If what I have said should not be plain enough, as I fear it
may not be, I will put you in the place where I began this series of
thoughts — I mean I began by seeing how man was formed by circumstances — and what are circumstances but touchstones of his
heart? and what are touchstones but provings of his heart, but fortifiers
or alterers of his nature? and what is his altered nature but his Soul?
— and what was his soul before it came into the world and had
these provings and alterations and perfectionings? — An intelligence
without Identity — and how is this Identity to be made? Through the
medium of the Heart? and how is the heart to become this Medium
but in a world of circumstances?

The letter forms an interesting commentary on so many
phases of Keats's thinking that there will not be space to
mention all. But we must pause briefly on some of the ideas
that suggest related aspects of his thought. For the poet, we
again must infer that the one way is to know the human heart,
and to *live*, to become able to feel the pulse-beat of a living
humanity. Concerning the powers and limitations of the
human mind, what Keats says here should be compared with
his own ideas as to the creative powers of the imagination

---

[7] Keats probably spent more time thinking of and discussing like matters than is usually supposed, as may be guessed from such casual remarks
as the following:

"I have been over to Dilke's this evening — there with Brown we have
been talking of different and indifferent Matters — of Euclid, of Meta-
phisics, of the Bible, of Shakespeare, of the horrid System and consequences
of the fagging at great schools."

— October, 1818. Forman. Vol. IV, p. 185.

and with the thought of others of his day. It is plain that the end toward which all things move is the creation of the human Mind, or Intelligence, or Soul. This not only makes the mind of man of tremendous importance, but it justifies a world of pains and troubles as necessary.[8] Only in such a world could the heart "feel and suffer" in the thousand diverse ways requisite to the molding of individual beings. Thus, even as Wordsworth proclaims "How exquisitely the Individual Mind" is fitted "to the external World," and "how exquisitely," in turn this "external World is fitted to the Mind," so Keats is here almost as sweepingly justifying the whole scheme of creation because it is so admirably designed for soul-making. In this, Keats has something in common, not only with Wordsworth, but with the main current of thought of his day, which, as Mr. Bradley says, evidenced "an unusually strong sense of the power and the possibilities of man or of the mind."[9] Yet Keats does not permit himself to fall into any of the absurdities that some of the thinkers of this school betrayed. He does go far with Wordsworth in his feeling —

> Not Chaos, not
> The darkest pit of lowest Erebus,
> Nor aught of blinder vacancy, scooped out
> By help of dreams, can breed such fear and awe
> As fall upon us often when we look
> Into our Minds, into the Mind of Man,
> My haunt and the main region of my song
> *(The Recluse,* ll. 788–794.)

But there is nothing of Fichte's wild extravagance in making man's mind not only the center but the creator and controller of the universe. Nor does he make the mistake of Schopen-

[8] "And through this pressure of the world upon them, souls recover their primitive unity with each other, and develop forms of life in which the absolute begins to show itself, and the particular soul to be fused and recast through larger experience, such as social self-sacrifice, art and science, or religion."
— Bosanquet. *The Value and Destiny of the Individual.*
[9] *English Poetry and German Philosophy,* p. 13.

hauer, who taught that the only means of escape from an intolerable world was through willing oneself away from it all, into a subjective region of aesthetic beauty. It is true that Keats does show at times a flash of something like Schopenhauer's will to aesthetic escape. It is plainly apparent in the *Ode to a Nightingale,* as we have seen. But he is too clearsighted to be deluded into a belief that the will of man can be so potent as to effect a permanent escape from the facts of life. He is ready to trust the imagination to create even greater things than the creator himself has made, when, as we have seen, these creations are based on the realities of the known world; but there is no escape from things as they are — " the nature of the world will not admit of it " — . . . " Let the fish philosophize the ice away " in winter time; let man exterminate the Poles and the sands of Africa, and whirlpools and volcanoes, then may he hope to be free from the " hardships and disquietudes " of existence. As Keats says in another place, " These things are," and there is no running away from them. Keats's direct argument is against the Godwin perfectibles in their belief that all our ills are due to manmade institutions and could be remedied by their abolition, and it strikes indirectly at the heart of all theories that exaggerate the possible capacities of the mind to change the world into whatever thing it would.

What shall be the ideal of the individual man in this " vale of Soul-making," so excellently fashioned to produce identities from the sparks thrown off by the God of the universe? We find Keats's answer in an earlier part of this same letter.[10] Man should adopt as his motto a " humble standard of disinterestedness," such as actuated the lives of Socrates and Jesus. This is a feeling that should " be carried to its highest pitch, as there is no fear of its ever injuring society — which it would do, I fear, if it were pushed to an extremity. For in wild nature the Hawk would lose his Breakfast of Robins and the Robin his of worms — the Lion must starve as well as the

[10] See Chapter VI, p. 97, where this letter is quoted at length.

Swallow. The greater part of Men make their way with the same instinctiveness, the same unwandering eye from their purposes, the same animal eagerness as the Hawk." It follows then that, even though life would be all upset by a too literal observance of the excellent ideal of disinterestedness, it yet remains the best standard for man to adopt: the conflict between his idealism and his native instincts will but lead to a desirable practicable compromise.

And so again the healthy element of balance and equilibrium in Keats's mental nature asserts itself. Disinterestedness is the ideal, but those very facts in the world that make it a fit place in which to develop souls — the necessity for direct " instinctive " pursuit of objects and the resultant struggle and hardship — would make a complete realization of this ideal impossible. " The life of Nature, he observes, depends on such pursuit carried indeed so far that it involves the destruction of one creature by another; and here, it will be noticed, he mentions those very proceedings of the hawk and the robin which had once horrified him and appeared incompatible with Beauty, but which now his philosophy has taught him to accept." [11] It is probably not altogether satisfactory, not quite complete, reconciliation, but such as it is, it suggests a progress toward a healthy philosophic attitude with some of the settled equanimity of spirit for which Keats so earnestly strove. For its effect upon his poetic life, we may turn to a continuation of the long journal letter in which these reflections on disinterestedness and the " vale of Soul-making " occur. It is fifteen days later,[12] and the *Ode to Psyche* is enclosed. It has been written, then, during the period of philosophic calm induced by these reasonings through which Keats

[11] Bradley: *Keats and " Philosophy."* *John Keats Memorial Volume*, p. 52. Mr. Bradley has treated this subject with his usual power and clearness. But he was simply making a few comments for the Memorial Volume and did not go into the matter exhaustively. There are times too when I cannot follow Mr. Bradley in his conclusions. Here, however, I am in perfect agreement.

[12] The section on " disinterestedness " was written March 19, that on the " vale of Soul-making " April 15. This is April 30, 1819.

had finally arrived at comparative peace with the world, in spite of all its horrid incongruities, and had found a justification for its suffering and misery. Here is Keats's comment:

> The following Poem — the last I have written — is the first and the only one with which I have taken even moderate pains. I have for the most part dash'd off my lines in a hurry.[13] This I have done leisurely — I think it reads the more richly for it, and will I hope encourage me to write other things in even a more peaceable and healthy spirit.

This poem then was done in "a peaceable and healthy spirit," obviously Keats's ideal for poetic composition. Is it too much to attribute that peace and health of mind to the recent philosophic triumph in reconciliation? The evidence indeed points that way. It is worth recalling too that between March and September of this year, all the great odes, beginning with the *Ode on Indolence,* evidently composed about March 19, and ending with the *Ode to Autumn,* September, 1819, had their origin. It is the period of Keats's nearest approach to philosophic resignation; it is also the period of his supreme poetic achievement.

I have pointed out that in the Vale of Soul-Making letter there is a clue as to Keats's metaphysical ideas — his notion that men originate as sparks of being thrown out from God, a conception of the universe as a unity — that we find borne out in other places in his writings. But inasmuch as this more strictly metaphysical phase of the " Mystery " was not of such pressing concern to Keats as were those more directly touching our immediate actualities, and inasmuch too as the

---

[13] In view of testimony we have from Bailey in regard to the writing of *Endymion* this statement seems a little questionable. Bailey says: " His mode of composition is best described by recounting our habits of study for one day during the month he visited me at Oxford. He wrote, and I read, sometimes at the same table, and sometimes at separate desks or tables, from breakfast to the time of our going out for exercise, — generally two or three o'clock. He sat down to his task, — which was about 50 lines a day, — with his paper before him, and wrote with as much regularity, and apparently as much ease, as he wrote his letters. . . . Sometimes he fell short of his allotted task, but not often. But he never forced himself." Houghton MSS. Quoted by Sidney Colvin in *John Keats,* p. 143.

poet's reflections on this problem are closely connected with his theory of Beauty, I defer consideration of them until we come to the chapter entitled *What is Beauty?* and shall here proceed to what seemed to be a more difficult problem with Keats than that of philosophic reconciliation: namely, the adjustment of his theory of detachment to his theory that the poet must concern himself with the vital matters of life, and the combination of them into an aesthetic that could comprehend both, and make each a complement to the other.

CHAPTER VI

DETACHMENT AND PHILOSOPHY — FURTHER
RECONCILIATION

WE have seen in the last chapter how knowledge and thought had led Keats to a place in his thinking where the " Burden of the Mystery " was eased in his acceptance of the world as it is, its pain and hardship a necessary part in the great scheme of " Soul-making." I wish now to show how he came to a further reconciliation of his theory of detachment, of poetry as aesthetic escape, with his conviction that the great poet must concern himself with humanity and the realities of life.

In Chapter IV I have shown that Keats had found that " philosophy," that is, knowledge and reason, might have a rightful place in poetry. Not only did it ease the " Burden of the Mystery," but it aided in sharpening the vision into the meaning of life. In the end, through the alchemy of the imaginative powers of the poet, the passions and affections of men may be almost etherealized; but in its inception, poetry must draw from the materials of life, made intelligible through the operation of reason and the intellect. But I also suggested there, that Keats did not find aesthetic peace in this apparent acceptance of philosophy, but that, probably owing to his difficulty in bringing himself to see how the imagination and the intellect might unite harmoniously, the old conflict still went on.

The letter and poems of late 1818 and all of 1819 contain much direct and indirect evidence of this conflict. The argument for philosophy is to be found in such passages as that in Keats's letter to George, March, 1819, where he is exclaiming: " Give me this credit, and you will not think that on my account I repeat Milton's lines —

> " How charming is divine Philosophy,
> Not harsh and crabbed, as dull fools suppose,
> But musical as is Apollo's lute."

No, not for myself, feeling grateful as I do to have got into a state of mind to relish them properly. Nothing ever becomes real until it is experienced — even a proverb is no proverb to you till life has illustrated it."

Then, in this same letter he confesses, " This is the very thing in which consists Poetry, and if so it is not so fine a thing as philosophy — for the same reason that an eagle is not so fine a thing as a truth." It was about this time, too, that he was declaring that he was determined to write no more except as a " running over " of knowledge and experience, — all of which might be taken as evidence of a decisive swing toward philosophy.

But one can find even stronger evidence condemning philosophy and exalting the dream world. There is, for example, the *Ode to a Nightingale*, with its decisive elevation of imaginative luxury and poetic escape; there is the *Ode on a Grecian Urn*, with its insistence on the authenticity of the imagination; and, finally, there are the oft-quoted lines from *Lamia*:

> Do not all charms fly
> At the mere touch of cold philosophy?

expressing apparent extreme revulsion against the philosophic.

The truth is, Keats had neither accepted nor rejected either philosophy or detachment to the exclusion of the other. He had been long engaged in a labyrinthian dispute with himself, in which he was earnestly seeking to reconcile his leaning toward the pure dream-world with the equally decisive urge toward the world of actuality and a philosophic understanding of it. In that conflict, sometimes the dream-world had the better of it, sometimes philosophy. But Keats never repudiated his early theory of poetic detachment; he never turned to a pursuit of " the Burden of the Mystery " or to any form of higher thought life whatever to the exclusion of his imaginative abstractions. Even those lines in the *Fall of Hyperion* which have of late been interpreted by Sir Sidney Colvin as a deep pessimistic revulsion against any but philosophic poetry and a special repudiation of the dreamer poet, read in their proper setting, do not at all show a discarding of the dream-world conception. Indeed the *Fall of Hyperion* is in itself a vision; it is captioned " A Vision "; the whole poem is set in as much of an otherworld atmosphere as is *Endymion* itself. The poet's vision in *Hyperion,* induced by the drinking of a magic potion, is a trance as genuine as the ecstatic soaring of the shepherd-prince in quest of his ideal Cynthia in the earlier work.

The real point is that Keats here makes plain that no aspirants can be admitted to the holy of holies of poetic insight except those who have first learned thoroughly the secrets of the human heart; he is simply uttering a profound anathema against mere visionaries, mere dreamers, those who would ascend into the realm of the ideal bearing no wisdom, no experiences, no knowledge of men. There are some contradictions in the passage, let us remember, and the lines have been too often explained without reference to these. Moreover, it has come to be taken for granted that the whole additional section in the Revision should be interpreted autobiographically, and that, forsooth, the aspiring poet here is Keats himself at the period in which he writes. This is probably not the case. Just as the shepherd-prince in *Endymion* is any poet, Keats no doubt had any poet in mind here. There is some very good evidence to show that one of Keats's ideals in poetry was that universals, not particulars, should be represented.[1] As to the contradictions I have mentioned let us read parts of the passage in question and study more closely its significance:

> " Those whom thou spakest of are no visionaries,"
>   Rejoin'd that voice; " they are no dreamers weak;
>   They seek no wonder but the human face,

[1] See the testimony of Reynolds in *What is Poetry?* Chapter X, page 199.

No music but a happy-noted voice:
They come not here, they have no thought to come;
And thou art here, for thou art less than they.
What benefit canst thou do, or all thy tribe,
To the great world? Thou art a dreaming thing,
A fever of thyself: think of the earth;
What bliss, even in hope, is there for thee?
What haven? every creature hath its home,
Every sole man hath days of joy and pain,
Whether his labours be sublime or low —
The pain alone, the joy alone, distinct:
Only the dreamer venoms all his days,
Bearing more woe than all his sins deserve.
Therefore, that happiness be somewhat shared,
Such things as thou art are admitted oft
Into like gardens thou didst pass erewhile;
And suffer'd in these temples: . . .

    .   .   .   .

Art thou not of the dreamer Tribe? [2]
The Poet and the dreamer are distinct
Diverse, sheer opposite, antipodes.
The one pours out a balm upon the World
The other vexes it." (Canto I, ll. 161–181.)

The inconsistency lies in this: The aspirant is condemned
as a weak, dreaming thing, belonging to a tribe at sheer antipodes from the poet kind; yet, take note, this dreamer, here,
now, *is* a poet; he has already entered the shrouded sanctuary
of high poetry, and that means that in the past he has been no
mere dreaming, fevered thing — for none can reach this height
but those " to whom the miseries of the world are misery " —
else he would have died on the pavement and "rotted there";
he has entered this sanctuary in a trance state; he is in a
dream world; and here his sight is cleared for the eternal
mysteries. The inconsistency is apparent. The one poetical
aspirant is playing at one and the same time both the rôle
of those mere weak visionaries who because they have no in-

[2] These last five lines are not in ordinary versions, but it appears they
should be. They were evidently cancelled by the publisher Woodhouse,
without full warrant. Vide de Selincourt. Notes, p. 518.

sight into life must be doomed to failure, and of those who by virtue of having drunk deep of the cup of earthly woes and sufferings are qualified to ascend the altar of poetic truth. Even though this were autobiographical it is obvious that Keats could not be both at once. At most there could be a condemnation only of what he once was in the thoughtless days, not of what he was now.

Now, admitting that Keats had attempted to do a hard thing in a hard way and had got a little tangled up in doing it, after all is not the general meaning clear? A mere dreaming poet is doomed to failure; but a dreaming poet made wise by earthly wisdom may reach the summit of poetic heights, where he may see and know all that it is in the power of human vision to discern. But this does not prove that Keats had discarded his theory of detachment in favor of philosophy; it only indicates that he had found a means of reconciling the two methods of poetic approach. The poet must still fly to his dream world, but in his flight he does not escape reality; rather he carries with him, to shape and inform his vision, the stored-up experiences of a life spent in sympathetic contact with his fellow-men.

How had this reconciliation come about? For answer we must turn to certain passages from Keats's writing on what I have chosen to call his more mature theory of detachment. Not that this theory originated in Keats's last years; on the contrary we see evidences of it as early as the spring of 1817. But the idea is one that seems to belong to riper intellect and to more highly developed thought than the early instinctive impulse to aesthetic escape. In one of the Marginalia found on a fly leaf of Keats's copy of *Troilus and Cressida,* an 1808 reprint of Shakespeare's folio of 1623, one finds this second type of detachment first suggested. This was probably written in the spring of 1817, for Keats was at that time carefully re-reading Shakespeare. " The genius of Shakespeare," he says, " was an innate universality — wherefore he had the utmost achievement of human intellect prostrate beneath his

indolent and kingly gaze. He could do man's utmost. His
plans of tasks to come were not of this world — if what he
purposed to do hereafter would not in his own Idea ' answer
the aim ' how tremendous must have been his conception of
the ultimates." Shakespeare was to Keats the high priest of
poetry, and what he saw in the great dramatist at this time
may be taken as his ideal. Here the goal for the poet is to be
able to rise above material things to a place where he may
look down from the heights of superior wisdom and insight
upon the affairs of this world. This gaze is to be " kingly "
and " indolent." The word " kingly " needs no explanation.
What Keats means by " indolent " may in part be inferred
from a passage in a later letter to his brothers, in which he
appears to be working around the same conception.

> . . . it struck me what quality went to form a man of achievement,
> especially in literature, and which Shakespeare possessed so enor-
> mously — I mean *Negative Capability*, that is, when a man is capable
> of being in uncertainties, mysteries, doubts, without any irritable
> reaching after fact and reason. Coleridge, for instance, would let go
> by a fine isolated verisimilitude caught from the Penetralium of
> mystery, from being incapable of remaining content with half-
> knowledge. This pursued through volumes would perhaps take us no
> further than this, that with a great poet the sense of Beauty over-
> comes every other consideration, or rather obliterates all consideration.

It is evidently from such expressions as this that Mr. G. R.
Elliott draws his conclusion that what Keats sought was " high
poetic repose." However, what Keats is seeking for is not
mere repose, but calm power, with all the surety and strength
that the knowledge of such power gives. Keats was too
dynamic to seek simple repose; he did, however, desire a self-
controlled capacity for contemplation. What he actually
craved was that easy, lofty, contemplative attitude which per-
mits the artist to see and know and express without the fever
of doubt and untempered emotion. The poet must be willing
to take the universe as he sees it, making use of his best perceptions without " irritable reaching out " after the unattain-

able, and that, even though his is only half-knowledge. This is " Negative Capability." A genius like Shakespeare, who " could do men's utmost with ease," had the capacity to lose himself completely in detached, contemplative, but penetrative absorption in the world and men; this was the secret of his great achievement.

There is ample proof that Keats strove for this serenity and calmness of spirit for himself. The ideal is suggested in the following:

Some think I have lost that poetical ardour and fire 'tis said I once had — The fact is, perhaps I have; but, instead of that, I hope I shall substitute a more thoughtful and quiet power. I am more frequently now contented to read and think, but now and then haunted with ambitious thoughts. Quieter in my pulse, improved in my digestion, exerting myself against vexing speculations, scarcely content to write the best verses for the fever they leave behind. I want to compose without this fever. I hope I one day shall.

Again he writes, " I have great hopes of success because I make use of my judgment more deliberately than I have yet done." And still more to the point is his comment on his *Ode to Psyche* quoted in the last chapter, to the effect that this poem was the first and only one with which he had taken even moderate pains, all his others having been written in a hurry; this one he had done leisurely, and hoped that it might read the more richly for it, and so probably encourage him to write other things " in a more peaceable and healthy spirit."

There are in the letters passages that help explain the nature of this attitude of contemplative detachment he craved. It seems that Keats was fond of imagining a supreme being as looking down upon this world, perceiving and interpreting all things with infinite understanding. In kind, this understanding is such as he as a poet possesses, but more infinite in scope. " Mrs. Tighe and Beattie once delighted me," he says, . . . " now I begin to see through them, and find nothing in them or ² weakness, and yet how many they still delight! Perhaps

    ² That is, " I now find nothing at all in them, or if I do see anything it is but weakness."

a superior being may look upon Shakespeare in the same light." The state of mind of this Being is that of a fine intellectual, impartial curiosity that analyzes, that may be amused by, the goings on in this world, but always understands and finds pleasure in them. There is much more in the following letter than illustration of the idea I am developing, but for the sake of coherence I must quote much that is not quite to the point. Keats did not set out to prove a proposition in logic when he wrote in one of his delightfully whimsical, philosophic veins to his friends. His letters are therefore full, as he once declared Shakespeare's sonnets to be, of " fine things said unintentionally," and reveal a lively mind at play or intense grapple as the case may be, with the thoughts that thronged its threshold; and rarely does he deny himself the luxury of a little side-excursion into some related subject wherever the paths of association lead. In their naïve ramifications, his reasonings might well become an interesting psychological study in the laws of association. But here is his letter as he wrote it:[3]

This morning I am in a sort of temper, indolent and supremely careless — I long after a stanza or two of Thomson's Castle of Indolence — my passions are all asleep, from my having slumbered till nearly eleven, and weakened the animal fibre all over me, to a delightful sensation, about three degrees this side of faintness. If I had teeth of pearl and the breath of lilies I should call it languor, but as I am[4] I must call it laziness. In this state of effeminacy the fibres of the brain are relaxed in common with the rest of the body, and to such a happy degree that pleasure has no show of enticement and pain no unbearable power. Neither Poetry, nor Ambition, nor Love have any alertness of countenance as they pass by me; they seem rather like figures on a Greek vase[5] — a Man and two women whom no one but myself could distinguish in their disguisement. This is the only happiness, and is a rare instance of the body overpowering the Mind.[6]

[3] To George and Georgiana Keats, March, 1819. Forman, Vol. V, p. 36.
[4] Keats's note: " Especially as I have a black eye."
[5] See the *Ode on Indolence,* probably written about this time — Colvin gives March, 1819 — for the same words and similar metaphors.
[6] Yet the whole letter shows how alertly the mind is at work. The fact is, it is the body that is quiescent.

I have this moment received a note from Haslam, in which he expects the death of his Father, who has been for some time in a state of insensibility; his mother bears up, he says, very well, — I shall go to town tomorrow to see him. This is the world — thus we cannot expect to give away many hours to pleasure. Circumstances are like Clouds, continually gathering and bursting. While we are laughing, the seed of some trouble is put into the wide arable land of events — while we are laughing it sprouts, it grows, and suddenly bears a poison fruit which we must pluck. Even so we have leisure to reason on the misfortunes of our friends; our own touch us too nearly for words. Very few men have ever arrived at a complete disinterestedness of Mind: very few have been influenced by a pure desire of the benefit of other, — in the greater part of the Benefactors of Humanity some meretricious motive has sullied their greatness — some melodramatic scenery has fascinated them. From the manner in which I feel Haslam's misfortune I perceive how far I am from any humble standard of disinterestedness. Yet this feeling ought to be carried to its highest pitch, as there is no fear of its ever injuring society — which it would do, I fear, pushed to an extremity. For in wild nature the Hawk would lose his Breakfast of Robins and the Robin his of Worms — the Lion must starve as well as the Swallow. The greater part of Men make their way with the same instinctiveness, the same unwandering eye from their purposes, the same animal eagerness as the Hawk. The Hawk wants a Mate, so does the Man — look at them both, they set about it and procure one in the same manner. They want both a nest and they both set about it in the same manner — they get their food in the same manner. The noble animal Man for his amusement smokes his pipe — the Hawk balances about the clouds — that is the only difference of their leisures. This it is that makes the Amusement of Life — to a speculative Mind — I go among the Fields and catch a glimpse of a Stoat or a fieldmouse peeping out of the withered grass — the creature hath a purpose, and its eyes are bright with it. I go amongst the buildings of a city and I see a man hurrying along — to what? the creature has a purpose and his eyes are bright with it. But then, as Wordsworth says, "we have all one human heart ——." (1) There is an electric fire in human nature tending to purify — so that among these human creatures there is continually some birth of new heroism. The pity is, that we must wonder at it, as we should at finding a pearl in rubbish. I have no doubt that thousands of people never heard of have had hearts completely disinterested: I can remember but two — Socrates and Jesus — Their histories evince it. What I heard a little time ago, Taylor observes with respect to

Socrates, may be said of Jesus — That he was so great a man that though he transmitted no writing of his own to posterity, we have his Mind and his sayings and his greatness handed to us by others. It is to be lamented that the history of the latter was written and revised by Men interested in the pious frauds of Religion. Yet through all this I see his splendour. Even here, though I myself am pursuing the same instinctive course as the veriest human animal you can think of, I am, however young, writing at random, straining at particles of light in the midst of a great darkness, without knowing the bearing of any one assertion, of any one opinion. Yet may I not in this be free from sin? May there not be superior beings, amused with any graceful, though instinctive, attitude my mind may fall into as I am entertained with the alertness of the Stoat or the anxiety of a Deer? Though a quarrel in the Streets is a thing to be hated, the energies displayed in it are fine; the commonest Man shows a grace in his quarrel. By a superior Being our reasonings may take the same tone — though erroneous they may be fine. This is the very thing in which consists Poetry, and if so it is not so fine a thing as philosophy — for the same reason that an eagle is not so fine a thing as a truth.

In this passage there is indicated much of what Keats must have meant by " Negative Capability." For a time the passions are asleep, the body is quiescent, and the mind, freed from the press of immediate demands, in a purely speculative mood indolently roams over the field of human experience. This state could come in its perfection only after the altar of poetic truth had been attained, at the stage of " innate universality." It could come too only after the misery of the world was deeply known. But the poet must not submerge himself in that misery. He must be able to send his being out like one of " God's spies," as it were, to partake in the existence of, and examine into, the heart of nature and all living things; but at the same time he must have the power to sit apart and contemplate in quiet mood and understand. He enters with gusto into the dark and bright phases of life, he enjoys both alike, because both end in speculation. He becomes a part of the identity of the sparrow under his window and " picks about the gravel " with him; the field-mouse and the stoat in their bright-eyed eagerness, man in his earnest haste to carry out his infinitely little purposes, all become objects of the poet's curious penetrative speculation. It is an analytical detached contemplation; yet it is warm and intimate; it may perceive much that is little and mean and ugly, but, because it has its genesis in the perfect knowledge of identification, it can see something fine in every action, something pleasing in every appearance. A quarrel in the streets is a thing to be hated, but the energies displayed are fine. These reasonings, defective as they are, may yet please a superior being who may take the same kind of pleasure in them that a man finds in the alertness of a stoat or the anxiety of a deer, that is, a speculative pleasure, a detached, intellectual enjoyment, which takes a relish in a thing for its own sake, that sees something fine even in the infirmities of men, the weakness of animals, and the cruelty of nature. "This is the very thing in which consists poetry." Objects in the world, actions, men — no matter how trivial or mean or ugly — become in themselves, apart from any moral relationships, of interest and value as subjects for poetry. That is why Keats is led frankly to admit that if this is true, poetry " is not so fine a thing as philosophy . . . for the same reason that an eagle is not so fine a thing as truth." Philosophy weighs with cold, analytical nicety, and judges on a basis of intrinsic and moral worth. Therefore her judgments should have the validity of reasoned conclusions based on all the facts. Poetry merely takes delight in revelation, in the interpretation of life as it is, on its own account, without any nice discrimination of ultimate values. But it is this very quality that makes poetry infinitely more desirable to Keats than is philosophy. Viewed in the abstract, philosophy may be a "finer thing than poetry," but, actually, — and one need only mention *To a Nightingale* and the *Ode on a Grecian Urn* to substantiate this statement — in its special province of illuminating life, poetry is to Keats unique and supreme. For Keats, the artist, philosophy has a place, but it is a means, not an end: its function is to prepare the intellect of the poet for its most significant and intensest adventures; in this capacity, it is indispensable to the greatest poetry, enriching its meanings, deepening its reach, and lending it, withal, the voice of authenticity and power.

Keats's ideal for the poetic nature would be realized, it would seem, in a serene, contemplative attitude of detachment, where, with ripe knowledge of the world and full ability to " think into the heart of humanity," the poet could yet see far beyond into the eternal universe of truth. He would be one to whom " the miseries of the world are misery," but who could yet assume toward men and all their " agony and strife " and toward all nature in its heartless, fierce destruction something of that attitude which a superior being might display in contemplation of the energies of man. Here indeed is suggested the " innate universality " and the ideal " Negative Capability " that Keats found his master Shakespeare to possess to such great degree, and which he so earnestly craved for himself. Detachment there still would be, but the poet would no longer go through the old oak forest " in a barren dream "; rather he would carry into that dream the sober wisdom of human thought and knowledge, and the steadying influence of a sympathetic understanding of the heart of man; the apparent break with the world would never be real, for always the dream would be enriched by the living presence of the palpitating actuality of the earth in a soul made wise by fellowship with its grief and pain. For Keats, the poet's realization of truth can come only through a harmonization of the whole realm of imaginative ideality with the visible world we know. The spirit of this imaginative world can be known and comprehended only through a vivid comprehension of this. The materials of the poetic imagination then are those of actuality as we know it, abstracted from its accidents of time and place, operated upon by the poet's intellect as certain chemicals operate upon a mass of neutral matter, and, so, transformed into symbols of universal truth and life. Finally, then, may we say, great poetry is of a world of its own, a world of abstractions, which yet draws its wisdom and its substance from the realm of the human heart. "The poetry of Lear, Othello, Cymbeline, etc., is the poetry of human passions and affections made almost ethereal by the power of the poet." The right region for poetry is the ethereal one, but it must be humanized by knowledge of the human heart, a knowledge great enough and complete enough to find its content in a state of abstracted, disinterested contemplation, which understands well enough the misery of the world, but "seeing all excellent and calculated toward a great whole," takes no part in the fret and fever of it all.

.   .   .   .

Thus far had Keats got in his reasoning on poetry and the poetic nature when he gave over his work. It is to be doubted whether he would have gone much further, or could have gone much further, in theory, had he lived to be three score and ten. His theory seems to be eminently satisfactory. It merely needs to be remarked that he came to his death before he had fully persuaded himself to an emotional acceptance of his reasoned judgment. We know how in *Lamia*, begun in July and finished in September, 1819, he berates the old bald-head philosopher and his lore, and we know how he confesses in later letters his impulses to untether fancy and let her run free. This all reflects a natural reaction toward the old first false love.

Sometimes, I like to read allegorical meaning into *Lamia*, and when I do, this is what I find: The ephemeral pleasure palace with its lustrous, high-arched halls, its wreaths of light perfume, and faery-roof upborne by nothing more than strains of haunting music, is the pleasure house of unreflective dreams of the young poet, who has lately met the seemingly beautiful Lamia, not truly beautiful, but false, a serpent in disguise — mere sensuous passion, feeling without knowledge, empty dreams. The young poet-lover Keats espoused her on a day; then came along "cold philosophy" — Keats's own unsparing domestic criticism, his awakening intellect and reason — and fixed him with his eye; then, not only did the false Duessa fade away, and the palace of barren dreams crumble, but the youngster who loved so unwisely also died [7] — though in his place was born a stronger, firmer soul, — but the Lamia story stops here.

[7] In sober criticism of *Endymion*, Keats wrote: "It is just that this youngster should die away." — Preface to *Endymion*.

CHAPTER VII

THE IMAGINATION

I

In both his letters and his poems Keats has, first to last, many things to say about the imagination. Always he understood it to be the supreme active principle in poetic composition. But how decisively with the rapid maturity of his intellect and critical judgment during the brief, fitful working period of his life did his ideas change and develop. Through the unquiet days and restless nights of burning thought, the puerile, vaporish notions of the 1815–1816 period became alchemized into sinewy convictions which, expressed in vigorous and picturesque language, stand as some of the most striking comments upon the nature of the imagination to be found in critical literature. In previous chapters I have pointed out how Keats's early notions of the ecstatic trance and "direct divination" methods of imaginative activity merged into the later more ripened conception of insight based on knowledge and experience. But in both of these views the imagination is all important as the vital element in poetic activity; Keats has merely arrived in his later thinking at a more comprehensive understanding of the intuitive faculties.

An analysis of his utterances on the subject from the middle of 1817 on, reveals that he has reached two significant conclusions as to the nature and function of the imagination. First, the imagination as an instrument of intuitive insight is the most authentic guide to ultimate truth; second, the imagination in its highest form is a generative force, in itself creative of essential reality.

II

Plato has said, "Not by wisdom do poets write, but by a sort of genius and inspiration." If by *wisdom* Plato means knowledge through reasoning, and I think he does, Keats would have been in complete agreement. For, though he believed firmly in the wisdom that springs from close contact with a harsh world and flowers into gracious human sympathy, Keats had no faith in mere cold knowledge and reason. "One of the first characteristics of the genuine and healthy poetic nature," declares Professor Shairp, "is this — it is rooted rather in the heart than in the head." So Keats thought. For to him poetry has its genesis in imagination, and feeling is both its rudder and its sails. Deep feeling makes possible thinking with our whole selves, soul and body. It emancipates the poet's mind from the incidental and temporary, leaving it free to probe the deeper mysteries of existence.

Imagination, with its springs in the heart rather than the head, though the head too has its place, becomes with Keats the highest and most authentic guide to truth. Not only is the imagination to be trusted more implicitly than reason in matters where both are operative, but there are even things clear to the imagination of which the reason knows nothing. As Joubert says, in words that well express Keats's thought on this subject, "Heaven, seeing that there were many truths which by our nature we could not know, and which it was to our interest, nevertheless, not to be ignorant of, took pity on us and granted us the faculty of imagining them."

"Keats," says James Russell Lowell, "certainly had more of the penetrative and sympathetic imagination which belongs to the poet, of that imagination which identifies itself with the momentary object of its contemplation, than any man of these later days." If this be true, Keats had realized in achievement one of his favorite poetic theories. For, supplementary to his demand for a detached state of spirit for poetic experience, was his conception of the poetic nature as a free entity with capacity to penetrate wherever it may choose, able to project itself into and merge itself in complete identification with the objects of its contemplation, yet in that mingling never losing its proper native qualities of unity and power.

In *Endymion,* torn by conflicting earthly and immortal loves, perplexed by a confusing, tangled web of circumstances, drawn by feeling and instinct in one direction, by reason in another, and, withal, carried out of himself by the power of his emotions, the poet cries out —

> What is this soul then? Whence
> Came it? It does not seem my own, and I
> Have no self-passion or identity.
>
> (Book IV, ll. 475–477.)

This is Keats himself speaking, uttering a thought that often came into his mind with the teasing interest of the novel and unexplained. " Nothing startles me beyond the moment," he declares to Bailey, evidently when thinking in this vein. " The Setting Sun will always set me to rights, or if a Sparrow come before my Window, I take part in its existence and pick about the gravel." Again he writes, " One of the most mysterious of semi-speculations is, one would suppose, that of one Mind's imagining into another." And these reflections at once suggest to our minds his definition of a poet —

> Where's the Poet? Show him! show him,
> Muses nine! that I may know him.
> 'Tis the man who with a man
> Is an equal, be he King,
> Or poorest of the beggar-clan,
> Or any other wondrous thing
> A man may be 'twixt ape and Plato;
> 'Tis the man who with a bird,
> Wren, or Eagle finds its way to
> All its instincts; he hath heard
> The Lion's roaring, and can tell
> What his horny throat expresseth,
> And to him the Tiger's yell
> Comes articulate and presseth
> On his ear like mother-tongue.

Through the power of the imagination, then, the poet is one who in spirit intimately lives with the feathered and wild creatures of the forest, who shares the identity of, hence, in thought and imagination, becomes equal to, king or beggar, or any that wear the semblance of man, and who, because he has partaken of the existence of bird or beast of prey, can understand the meaning of its every move or cry.

In a second passage in *Endymion*, there is suggested the other imaginative extreme — from the very earthy, we ascend at a leap to the ethereal. " Wherein lies happiness? " the poet has asked. It is, he replies, in that which raises our ready minds to a " fellowship with essence," leaving us completely " alchemized and free of space."

> Feel we these things? — that moment have we stept
> Into a sort of oneness, and our state
> Is like a floating spirit's. But there are
> Richer entanglements, enthralments far
> More self-destroying, leading, by degrees,
> To the chief intensity.
>
> (Book I, 795–800.)

Here plainly is implied a complete identity with the infinite, when the mind of the poet shall merge itself imaginatively into the spirit of the universe, to lose itself in a divine " fellowship with essence."

In a self-revelatory letter to Richard Woodhouse, written October 27, 1818, Keats presents further evidence. Here we find that this power of identification is reciprocal; not only does the poet's self go out to others, but the identity of others forces itself upon him, until he is helpless before its might:

1st. As to the poetical character itself (I mean that sort, of which, if I am anything, I am a member; that sort distinguished from the Wordsworthian, or egotistical Sublime; which is a thing per se, and stands alone), it is not itself — it has no self — It is everything and nothing. It has no character — it enjoys light and shade; it lives in gusto,[1] be it foul or fair, high or low, rich or poor, mean or elevated. —

---

[1] Tragic poetry, Hazlitt declares, " has its source and ground-work in a common love of excitement." — *On Poetry in General*.

It has as much delight in conceiving an Iago as an Imogen.[2]   What shocks the virtuous philosopher delights the chameleon poet. It does no harm from its relish of the dark side of things, any more than from its taste for the bright one, because they both end in speculation. A poet is the most unpoetical of anything in existence, because he has no Identity — he is continually in for and filling some other body. The Sun, — the Moon, — the Sea, and men and women, who are creatures of impulse, are poetical, and have about them an unchange-able attribute; the poet has none, no identity — he is certainly the most unpoetical of all God's creatures. — If then he has no self, and if I am a poet, where is the wonder that I should say I would write no more?   Might I not at that very instant have been cogitating on the Characters of Saturn and Ops?   It is a wretched thing to confess; but it is a very fact, that not one word I ever utter can be taken for granted as an opinion growing out of my identical Nature — How can it, when I have no Nature?   When I am in a room with people, if I ever am free from speculating on creations of my own brain, then, not myself goes home to myself, but the identity of every one in the room begins to press upon me, so that I am in a very little time an-nihilated — not only among men; it would be the same in a nursery of Children.

Keats's conception is that the poet's being is a sort of de-tached entity — an unfettered spirit-like thing — independent of earthy circumstances and vision, free to take leave of the body to roam about where it will, penetrating into the mys-terious chambers of the soul's deepest recesses, or, soaring into the shadowy and illimitable spaces of the universe, to mingle with " essence " in " fellowship divine "; its de-light is ever fresh, adventurous speculation, whether down into the darker regions of existence or up into the majestic realm of " Saturn and old Ops."   This process with Keats is not merely a submergence of one's self into another; it is not a substitution where the poet puts himself in the place of the object of his contemplation: it is rather a sort of etherized penetration, in which the poetic soul, acting as

---

[2] Note Hazlitt's words: " Poetry is only the highest eloquence of pas-sion, the most vivid form of expression that can be given to our concep-tion of anything, whether pleasurable or painful, mean or dignified, de-lightful or distressing." — On Poetry in General.

an ethereal chemical operating on man and the physical world, liberates the fine essence of spiritual being in its purest and freest state, to be condensed, through the agency of beautiful verse, into new elements of living truth. " Men of Genius," declares Keats, writing to Bailey, " are great as certain ethereal Chemicals operating on the Mass of neutral intellect — but they have not any individuality, any determined Character."

The remarks on the reciprocal phase of identity are an interesti ıg commentary on the insistence with which life crowded itself upon Keats. Whether he would or no, the personalities about him pressed upon him, absorbed him, annihilated him.

How far may a poet's utterances be taken as expressing himself? Keats would seem to say, " Not in the least "; for, except in the rare instances of the " Wordsworthian egotistical sublime," the true poet has no permanent identity to express, and therefore cannot, if he would, lay bare the rooms of his house, nor can he with sonnet or any other key unlock his own heart. Elsewhere Keats declares, " The only means of strengthening one's intellect is to make up one's mind about nothing — to let the mind be a thoroughfare for all thoughts, not a select party." What type of mind better fitted for this thoroughfare than that of a poet who has no self-identity, but whose penetrative mind can roam whither it will, can see and apprehend all clearly, and bring home its fruits of truth untainted by bias or prejudice? Is it not a pleasing thought that the mind of the greatest poet may be a sort of filter through which the great truths of the eternal universe are clarified, organized, and given to the world? Keats's logic would lead one to consider the poet as so closely identifying himself with his object, his own identity being submerged, that his utterance really becomes a true and unhampered expression of the object itself. Keats " does not put himself on an equality " with Nature, says Reynolds. " You do not see him, when you see her.[3] " This seems to be Keats's ideal —

[3] Alfred, West of England Journal. Quoted in Forman. Vol. IV, p. 178.

to represent things as they are without putting himself into the picture.

To such a poet, able to imagine himself into any living thing, mere life itself and the things of life that lead to speculation are alone adequate to pleasurable activity. So he knows no good and evil; he is as delighted to contemplate and portray the villainy of an Iago as to share in and represent the white virtue of an Imogen. For each one embodies life and a bit of the passion and truth of life, and for a poet that is enough.

I have already quoted from the famous letter on the Imagination written to Bailey in November, 1817.[4] But Keats's discussion here is so crowded with suggestions as to the nature, function, and importance of the imaginative activity that I wish to include a longer extract. In this passage Keats addresses himself directly to the subject, and his observations are of all the worth that a real thinker's unpremeditated, spontaneous utterance on any subject close to his heart always is — utterance where we arrive at the crux of a matter directly without the sophistications of studied delivery.

But I am running my head into a subject which I am certain I could not do justice to under five Years' study, and 3 vols. octavo — and, moreover, long to be talking about the Imagination . . . O! I wish I was as certain of the end of all your troubles as that of your momentary start about the authenticity of the Imagination. I am certain of nothing but of the holiness of the Heart's affections, and the truth of Imagination! What the Imagination seizes as Beauty must be Truth — whether it existed before or not, — for I have the same idea of all our passions as of Love: they are all, in their sublime, creative of essential Beauty. In a Word, you may know my favorite speculation by my first Book,[5] and the little Song I sent in my last, which is a representation from the fancy of the probable mode of operating in these Matters. The Imagination may be compared to

[4] See Chapter IV, p. 64.
[5] The first book of *Endymion*. The song was lost. Colvin writes, " Of ' my last,' that is of his preceding letter to Bailey, unhappily but a fragment is preserved, and the song must have been lost with the sheet or sheets which went astray." Page 156.

Adam's dream, — he awoke and found it truth: [6] — I am more zealous in this affair, because I have never yet been able to perceive how anything can be known for truth by consecutive reasoning — and yet it must be. Can it be that even the greatest Philosopher ever arrived at his Goal without putting aside numerous objections? However, it may be, O for a life of Sensations [7] rather than of Thoughts! It is " a Vision in the form of Youth," a shadow of reality to come — and this consideration has further convinced me, — for it has come as auxiliary to another favorite speculation of mine, — that we shall enjoy ourselves hereafter by having what we called happiness on Earth repeated in a finer tone. And yet such a fate can only befall those who delight in Sensation, rather than hunger as you do after Truth.[8] Adam's dream will do here, and seems to be a Conviction that Imagination and its empyreal reflexion, is the same as human life and its spiritual repetition. But, as I was saying, the simple imaginative Mind may have its rewards in the repetition of its own silent Working coming continually on the Spirit with a fine Suddenness.[9] To compare great things with small, have you never, by being surprised with an old Melody, in a delicious place by a delicious voice, *felt* over again your very speculations and surmises at the time it first operated on your soul? do you not remember forming to yourself the Singer's face — more beautiful than it was possible, and yet, with the elevation of the Moment, you did not think so? Even then you were mounted on the Wings of Imagination, so high that the prototype must be hereafter — that delicious face you will see. . . . Sure this can not be exactly the case with a complex mind — one that is imaginative, and at the same time careful of its fruits, — who would exist partly on Sensation, partly on thought — to whom it is necessary that " years should bring the philosophic Mind? " Such a one I consider yours, and therefore it is necessary to your eternal happiness that you not only drink this old Wine of Heaven, which I shall call the redigestion of our most ethereal Musings upon Earth, but also increase in knowledge, and know all things.

Here Keats is confessing, perhaps to the point of exaggeration, his complete faith in the authenticity of the imagination.

---

[6] *Paradise Lost.* VIII, ll. 288–311, or, more likely, VIII, ll. 452–490.
See Colvin, p. 155.
[7] Let us remember that Keats means by " Sensations " intuitive imagination.
[8] That is, factual and reasoned knowledge.
[9] Sidney Colvin's comments on the meaning of this letter are valuable.
See *John Keats,* pp. 154–155.

It is a faith that wavers somewhat in the mental shake-up of 1818, when the young poet's conception of what constitutes imagination is altered as he perceives ever more and more that barren dreams are vain and breed only mawkishness in verse; but even when under the influence of the insistent conviction that a poet must understand the " Mystery," and must know life to the core, Keats perceives that the final way to great poetry is through the imagination. Milton was his exemplar in philosophic attainment; yet when he writes in the very spiritual presence of the " old scholar of the spheres," he still adheres to his faith in the intuitive as the last resort for poets:

> But vain is now the burning and the strife
> Pangs are in vain, until I grow high-rife
>   With old Philosophy,
> And mad with glimpses of futurity.
>
> (*On a Lock of Milton's Hair*)

To grow "high rife with old philosophy " is only a preparation for, and an accompaniment of, the highest type of seer-like vision — the vision of a prophet to whom all veils are rent in " glimpses of futurity."

This does not mean that Keats would in the end minimize the importance of knowledge. He came to see that for the poet every avenue to the fullest and most complete knowledge of reality should be left open. He realized, as Mr. Herford, in his *Is There a Poetic View of the World?*, puts it, that " What distinguishes poetic from religious or philosophic apprehension is not that it turns away from reality, but that it lies open to and in eager watch for reality at doors and windows which with them are barred or blind. The poet's soul resides, so to speak, in his senses, in his emotions, in his imagination, as well as in his conscious intelligence; and we may provisionally describe poetic apprehension as an intense state of consciousness in which all these are concerned." Most of this Keats understood when he wrote this letter. His instinct taught him that the doors and windows to reality barred to the scientists and philosopher — men of "consecutive minds" — are the very ones the poet most uses, those of "Sensation," or intuitive perception; only at this time he had not yet realized the importance of "his conscious intelligence." That was to come when he should grow to see the necessity for the "gradual ripening of all the intellectual powers."

One word that follows is used carelessly and is confusing: "And yet such a fate can only befall those who delight in sensation, rather than hunger as you do after Truth." But taken in connection with the preceding sentences, it appears that it is truth from reason alone that is meant, without respect to imaginative truth, and this, of course, is quite consistent with Keats's whole thought.

Santayana has shown in his admirable way the right relation between reasoning and philosophy and poetry:

In philosophy itself investigation and reasoning are only preparatory and servile parts, means to an end. They terminate in insight, or what in the noblest sense of the word may be called *theory*, θεωρια, — a steady contemplation of all things in their order and worth. Such contemplation is imaginative. No one can reach it who has not enlarged his mind and tamed his heart. A philosopher who attains it is, for the moment, a poet; and a poet who turns his practised and passionate imagination on the order of all things, or on anything in the light of the whole, is for the moment a philosopher.[10]

This is a doctrine to which Keats would have heartily subscribed. For in this larger sense he was always an intuitionist. The imaginative is the highest, and most generative, of all poetic functions. Reason and knowledge are requisites, it is true; but only as educators of the imagination. They are but guides to point the way. In the end the pupil far outruns the master.

In his eager pursuit of truth Keats believed that intuitive insight rather than reason is to be trusted as the authentic

[10] *Three Philosophic Poets*, p. 10.

guide to the hidden mysteries of the poetic world. To sound the sea of imaginative reality to the depths was the passionate longing of his soul. To see, to know, as did Shakespeare, Milton, Homer,— such was his young Parnassian dream. And he believed the magic open sesame to all the fair realms beyond to be the feelings, refined and spiritualized into poetic imagination. We recognize this ideal in these lines to Homer:

> Standing aloof in giant ignorance,
> Of thee I hear and of the Cyclades,
> As one who sits ashore and longs perchance
> To visit dolphin-coral in deep seas.
> So thou wast blind! — but then the veil was rent;
> For Jove uncurtain'd Heaven to let thee live,
> And Neptune made for thee a spermy tent,
> And Pan made sing for thee his forest-hive;
> Aye, on the shores of darkness there is light,
> And precipices show untrodden green;
> There is a budding morrow in midnight, —
> There is a triple sight in blindness keen;
> Such seeing hadst thou, as it once befel
> To Dian, Queen of Earth, and Heaven, and Hell.

The poet is one before whose insistent spirit the veils of heaven are rent; through the power of imagination — for what else can be this " triple sight in blindness keen? " — the poet has power to ascend into the empyrean or to find a home in the bottomless depths of the ocean; his seeing is like that of the gods, to whom all things, in " Earth and Heaven and Hell," are clear. Reason could not do this. All his lifetime Keats earnestly, passionately, sought truth, but not truth through reason alone. Reason could never carry a poet to the heart of man,

> Be he King
> Or poorest of the beggar clan,

nor help him find his way to all the instincts of bird, wren, or eagle; and reason could never uncurtain " heaven," nor guide in exploring the " passages all dark " that lead to the inner

" Penetralium " of the " Burden of the Mystery," where the miseries and agonies of the world are bared. Keats could not trust reason to reveal ultimate reality to him.

It was this instinctive conviction which Keats held from the very first that prompted his almost savage attack in *Sleep and Poetry* upon the classical poets and their verse of reason and good taste. It evolved naturally from his reflections on the place of intuition and feeling in poetry; he could not help contrasting the high imaginative power of the older poetry with its decline in the verse of poets like Boileau and Pope. He insists upon a return to imagination:

> Is there so small a range
> In the present strength of manhood, that the high
> Imagination can not freely fly
> As she was wont of old? . . .
> . . . Has she not shown us all?
> From the clear space of ether, to the small
> Breath of new buds unfolding? From the meaning
> Of Jove's large eye-brow, to the tender greening
> Of April meadows? Here her altar shone,
> E'en in this isle;[11] and who could paragon
> The fervid choir that lifted up a noise
> Of harmony, to which it aye will poise
> Its mighty self of convoluting sound
> Huge as a planet, and like that roll round,
> Eternally around a dizzy void.

And then follows the indignant denunciation:

> Could all this be forgotten? Yes, a schism
> Nurtured by foppery and barbarism,
> Made great Apollo blush for this his land.

There came a time when the highest honors were paid to men who had not the slightest understanding of real poetry; but in sublime self-deception,

[11] In the imaginative poetry of Chaucer, Spenser, Shakespeare, and Milton.

> . . . with a puling infant's force
> They sway'd about upon a rocking horse,
> And thought it Pegasus. Ah, dismal soul'd!
> The winds of heaven blew, the ocean roll'd
> Its gathering waves — ye felt it not. The blue
> Bared its eternal bosom and the dew
> Of summer nights collected still to make
> The morning precious: beauty was awake!
> Why were ye not awake? But ye were dead
> To things ye knew not of, — were closely wed
> To musty laws lined out with wretched rule
> And compass vile: so that ye taught a school
> Of dolts to smooth, inlay, and clip, and fit,
> Till, like the certain wands of Jacob's wit,
> Their verses tallied. Easy was the task:
> A thousand handicraftsmen wore the mask
> Of Poesy. Ill-fated, impious race!
> That blasphemed the bright Lyrist to his face,
> And did not know it, — no, they went about
> Holding a poor, decrepid standard out
> Mark'd with most flimsy mottos, and in large
> The name of one Boileau!
>
> (*Sleep and Poetry*, ll. 181–201.)

Here Keats expresses his allegiance to freedom-giving, truth-revealing intuitive imagination as the informing spirit of poetry, and his deep-rooted antagonism to the idea of verse coldly thought out, cut by feet and chiseled by rule, all unwarmed by the penetrative fires of feeling. In this the young poet is much in accord with the poetic thought of his day. In these lines there are distinct echoes of Wordsworth's sonnet beginning " The World is too much with us," with its emphasis upon a fresh imaginative enjoyment of beauty; and there is expressed the same impatience of studied formalism in art that Wordsworth voices in his " A Poet! He hath put his heart to school " —

> A Poet! He hath put his heart to school,
> Nor dares to move unpropped upon the staff
> Which Art hath lodged within his hand — must laugh
> By precept only, and shed tears by rule.

Thy Art be Nature; the live current quaff,
And let the groveller sip his stagnant pool,
In fear that else when Critics grave and cool
Have killed him, scorn should write his epitaph.

But Keats is not merely echoing Wordsworth. Young as he is, he is declaring what was to him from first to last a basic tenet of his poetic creed. To follow the teachings of Boileau, he instinctively felt, would be to take the surest possible route to artistic blight and stultification. To put such reins upon the poetic faculties as the classical school proposed was, to him, to falsify nature and to destroy the imagination.

Yet, Keats and Boileau agreed on one essential: each knew that nothing is more dangerous than for a poet to write with the imagination only; Boileau believed this firmly, and Keats, at least after 1818, came to know that the highest poetry could not be written in this way. But Keats took the more balanced view. Where Boileau would make the imagination subordinate, Keats would have the imagination and the intellect work together, like twin sisters, as it were, except that the imaginative sister should have the stronger, clearer eyes and the deeper, more accurate seeing power, and so should always be the authority in case of dispute. In fact Keats refused to trust the intellectual sister's vision at all until he had appealed to the imaginative twin to corroborate her judgment — " I can never be sure of a truth except by a clear conception of its beauty." On the other hand he will even discredit or ignore the intellect if the imagination's penetrative vision has pierced some misty haze and caught gleams that her slower sister's eye cannot detect: " What the Imagination seizes as beauty must be truth." Boileau's mistake, as Brunetière points out in a statement with which Keats would agree, is that he failed to " recognize that, in spite of all its excesses, the imagination, that is to say the faculty of transcending nature, of even seeing in it what is not there, provided only that he make us see it, that imagination remains the supreme faculty of the poet, his original aptitude, one whose place can be supplied by no other, without which one may indeed be artist, writer, orator, but never poet — for this it is we are bound to upbraid him. The reason is that he himself was not a poet. . . ." [12]

So it was not that Keats discarded knowledge; we have seen how earnestly he sought to know and understand: it was not that he despised conscious craftsmanship in verse building; we shall see how much thought he himself gave to fitting form for poetic substance: it was simply that he felt that without the operation of the imagination there could be no artistic perception nor revelation. In the education of the imagination, all knowledge and intellect have a place. But Keats would maintain firmly with Leigh Hunt that "thought by itself makes no poetry at all." [13] For the conclusions of the understanding can at best be only so many matters of fact. "Sensation," on the other hand, in that it gives a sense of deepest truth through direct emotionalized intuition, is a fundamental to all real poetry; though without knowledge as a ballast, it leads to lack of balance, and to irresponsible, giddy soaring. In other words, "sensation" without knowledge is mere fancy, with knowledge it becomes creative imagination, the basis of all true art.

And now we come to those other lines that are so often quoted to show how Keats elevated the "paradise of the sensations over the mind":

> . . . Do not all charms fly
> At the mere touch of cold philosophy?
> There was an awful rainbow once in heaven:
> We know her woof, her texture; she is given
> In the dull catalogue of common things.
> Philosophy will clip an angel's wings,
> Conquer all mysteries by rule and line,
> Empty the haunted air, and gnomed mine —
> Unweave a rainbow, as it erewhile made
> The tender-person'd Lamia melt into a shade.
>
> (*Lamia.* II, ll. 229–238.)

---

[12] *L'Esthétique de Boileau* in the *Revue des deux Mondes*, 93, 1889. Quoted in Cook's *Art of Poetry*, p. L.   [13] *Imagination and Fancy*, p. 63.

It is possible to interpret this passage by the application of a fact earlier developed in this treatise — the fact that Keats had a sort of dual nature, one half of which cried for the untrammeled sway of instinctive creative fancy, the other of which turned toward wisdom and knowledge.

But there is a more satisfactory explanation. We must interpret the passage in the light of all that Keats says elsewhere. Then it is cold " reason unmitigated by the warmth of intuitive imagination " that Keats condemns, as he does always. Just as we have seen that feeling or " sensation " by itself is not enough until balanced by reason and knowledge, so " cold philosophy " out of sympathy with the human heart and natural beauty he as a poet rightly despises. As Goethe declares, the Significant " must have a soul breathed into it before it can be art."

Keats realized that poetry has a peculiar province of knowledge all her own, her proper realm being the imaginative as opposed to the scientific. He probably felt as he may have heard Hazlitt declare in his lectures of the spring of 1818, that the progress of scientific knowledge and refinement has a tendency to circumscribe the limits of the imagination, and " to clip the wings of poetry." Jacob's dream was a product of imagination, but, says Hazlitt, " There can never be another Jacob's dream. Since that time, the heavens have gone farther off, and grown astronomical." Hard, dry, scientific fact, then, must be indeed antagonistic to poetry. But that does not apply to " philosophy " in its broader sense of spiritual wisdom and knowledge of humanity. On the contrary, a proper union of this sort of philosophy with feeling and sensation becomes imagination, the great revealer of poetic truth. " What then shall we say? " inquires Coleridge. " Even this; that Shakespeare, no mere child of nature; no automaton of genius; no passive vehicle of inspiration, possessed by the spirit, not possessing it; first studied patiently, meditated deeply, understood minutely, till knowledge, become habitual and intuitive, wedded itself to his habitual feelings, and at length gave birth to that stupendous power by which he stands alone, with no equal or second in his own class." It was such a power as this that Keats longed to possess; and had he lived who knows but that finally he would have realized his dream.

III

Keats's poetic world was an imaginative one. Byron " describes what he sees," he declared, " I describe what I imagine. Mine is the hardest task." This was written in September, 1819, just when Keats was at the peak of his poetic powers, and may be trusted as a final utterance. Keats was not in any sense confessing that the objects of his verse were lacking one whit of the reality to be found in Byron's; indeed he would have contended that his own poetry reflected the greater truth and reality, in that his was universal, while Byron's was only particular. Keats believed that the imagination of the true poet was capable not only of perceiving, but of creating essential reality. Sometimes it appears that he thinks of this imaginative power as extending to the point of actual new creations, as when he boldly announced, " What the Imagination seizes as Beauty must be Truth whether it existed before or not." At other times, it would seem that he has reference to a re-creative force able to seize visible materials and truth that lies hidden and combine them into new forms, as when he writes in elevated vein of his " readiness to measure time by what is done and to die in six hours could plans be brought to conclusions — the looking upon the Sun, the Moon, the Stars, the Earth and its contents, as materials to form greater things — that is to say ethereal things — but here I am talking like a Madman — greater things than our Creator himself made." Keats would logically hold that true art, the product of this generative power of the mind, embodies both the visible sensuous and the generative unseen spiritual, combined in a single imaginative creation. In this Keats is Hegelian. Note Hegel's own comment:

Genuine reality is only to be found beyond the immediacy of feeling and of external objects. Nothing is genuinely real but that which
is actual in its own right, that which is the substance of nature and
of mind, fixing itself indeed in present and definite existence, but in
this existence still retaining its essential and self-centered being, and
thus and no otherwise attaining genuine reality. . . . Art liberates the
real import of appearances from the semblance and deception of this
bad and fleeting world, and imparts to phenomenal semblances a
higher reality, born of mind. The appearances of art, therefore, far
from being mere semblances, have the higher reality and the more
genuine existence in comparison with the realities of common life.

With Keats the essential reality of these imaginative conceptions was not at all dependent on their expression in art
forms; it was only necessary for them to exist in the mind of
the poet, who, beginning with the appearances of men and
things, constructs for himself a world of his own, which includes but transcends the things of sense. " What creates the
pleasure of not knowing? " Keats reflects, as he reads Book I
of *Paradise Lost*. " A sense of independence, of power, from
the fancy's creating a world of its own by the sense of prob-
abilities," he replies.

There is no room to doubt Keats's conviction as to the
capacity of the imagination to create spiritual reality. It is
made evident in the letter concerning the " mighty abstract
idea of beauty," where the poet declares that he feels more
and more as his imagination strengthens that he does " not live
in this world alone but in a thousand worlds "; the idea is
clearly conveyed in the passages just quoted — in his explanation that where Byron describes the visible, he describes what
he imagines; in his epigrammatic " What the imagination
seizes as Beauty must be Truth for I have the same idea of
all our passions as of Love, they are all in their sublime creative of essential beauty "; in his declaration that the poet
has power to create " ethereal things greater than those of
the Creator himself " — and it is even more explicitly stated
in the following:

I want to hear very much whether Poetry and literature in general
has gained, or lost interest with you — and what sort of writing is of
the highest gust with you now. With what sensation do you read
Fielding? — and do not Hogarth's pictures seem an old thing to you?
Yet you are very little more removed from general association than
I am — recollect that no Man can live but in one society at a time —
his enjoyment in the different states of human society must depend
upon the Powers of his Mind — that is you can imagine a Roman
triumph or an Olympic game as well as I can. We with our bodily
eyes see but the fashion and Manners of one country for one age —
and then we die. Now to me manners and customs long since passed
whether among the Babylonians or the Bactrians, are as real, or even
more real than those among which I now live. My thoughts have
turned lately this way. The more we know the more inadequacy we
find in the world to satisfy us — this is an old observation; but I
have made up my Mind never to take anything for granted — but
even to examine the truth of the commonest proverbs.

In such passages as these we not only discover a complete
confession of Keats's idealism, but we find revealed the important function of the imagination in combining and creating
into forms of beauty the truths that lie beyond the visible.
The world of sense is imperfect and incomplete: " The more
we know the more inadequacy we find in the world to satisfy
us." Therefore, every appearance must be scrutinized for its
possible implications as to the larger reality. Perceptions of
this reality can come only through the operation of the imaginative faculty; only through the imagination can the poet
see the world true and see it whole, and only through the
imagination can he create and re-create new forms of beauty.
This holds in the realm of imaginative literature and history
as well as in relation to the real and ideal worlds; and the
capacity to create is largely independent of time or place or
circumstances. George and Georgiana Keats are in remote
America; yet — " recollect that no man can live but in one
society at a time — that is, you can imagine a Roman triumph
or an Olympic game as well as I can." Man's real ability to
know life to the full rests upon the resources of his imagination. Art treasures and general cultural environment are not

necessary to the fullest appreciation of the beauty of the world. Give a man the gift of imagination, and in the Sahara desert as well as London the whole universe is at his command. Roman and Egyptian civilizations long since melted away, are re-created at the call of this divine faculty, and form a portion of the aggregate of all reality to make an ideal whole.

From what has just been said it is evident that the creative power of the imagination is in no wise restricted by inability to see with the physical eyes that which it creates or the materials with which it works. This fact is thrown into stronger relief by a suggestive remark Keats made concerning Milton, occurring in a note on the early lines of *Paradise Lost*. "A poet," declares Keats, "can seldom have justice done to his imagination — for men are as distinct in their conceptions of material shadowings as they are in matters of spiritual understanding: it can scarcely be conceived how Milton's blindness might here aid the magnitude of his conceptions as a bat in a large gothic vault." Keats's statement is incomplete, yet as Mr. Forman has pointed out (Volume III, page 258), the general sense is clear. Milton is working with vast conceptions, the materials for which are visible only to the imaginative eye. How are such transcendent conceptions to be accounted for? Keats's suggestion is " that Milton's blindness might so sharpen his imagination as to give him the same advantage in the realm of the unseen as a bat has in the darkness of a gothic vault," that is, the ability to imagine ultimates — infinite spaces peopled by personages of infinite scope and power.

" Imagination then," says Professor Mackail, in his *Lectures on Poetry*, " is the power or faculty which creates, in so far as creation is within human power. It is the likeness or echo of the divine creative power; like it, according to its measure, it gives shape and substance to what had neither, what was without form and void.[14] It dissolves in order to re-create,

[14] " Must not the imagination weave garments, visible bodies, wherein the else invisible creations and inspirations of our reason are, like spirits revealed. . . ." Carlyle: *Sartor Resartus*.

or if the word create be too strong, to unify and idealize."
This perhaps would sum up fairly well Keats's thoughts as to
the creative imagination. He would have added, as he matured
in intellect, that the authenticity of these creations must be
governed by the extent to which the poet knows the world
of men.

But the creations of the imagination are none the less real
because they are thus limited. No, " What the imagination
seizes as beauty must be truth, whether it existed before or
not." That is, what the imagination constructs for itself as
reality is truth. Note the real significance of certain phrases
in the letter quoted: " Now to me manners and customs long
since passed, whether among the Babylonians or the Bactrians,
are as real, or even more real than those among which I now
live." " Even more real," Keats says, for he ever trusted to
the light of imagination more fully than to the voice of reason.
And things imagined are never reasoned; they are felt. To
Keats, things of the mind, creations of the imagination, were
as real as to Wordsworth when he wrote:

> Paradise, and groves
> Elysian, Fortunate Fields, like those of old
> Sought in the Atlantic Main — why should they be
> A history only of departed things.
> Or a mere fiction of what never was?
> For the discerning intellect of Man,
> When wedded to this goodly universe
> In love and holy passion, shall find these
> A simple produce of the common day.
>
> (*The Recluse*, ll. 799–808.)

In his *Sartor Resartus*, Carlyle has most vigorously and
succinctly expressed a similar idea:

To clap on your felt, and, simply by wishing you were Any*where*,
straightway to be *There!* Next to clap on your other felt, and,
simply by wishing you were Any*when*, straightway to be *Then!*
This were indeed the grander: shooting at will from the *Fire-Creation*
of the World to its Fire-Consummation; here historically present in

the first century, conversing face to face with Paul and Seneca; there prophetically in the Thirty-first, conversing also face to face with other Pauls and Senecas, who as yet stand hidden in the depths of that late Fire.

Or thinkest thou it were impossible, unimaginable? Is the Past annihilated then, or only past; is the Future non-extant, or only future? Those mystic faculties of thine, Memory and Hope, already answer: already through those mystic avenues, thou the Earth-blinded summonest both Past and Future, and communist with them, though as yet darkly, and with mute beckonings. The curtains of Yesterday drop down, the curtains of tomorrow roll up; but Yesterday and Tomorrow both *are.* Pierce through the time-element, glance into the Eternal, Believe what thou findest written in the sanctuaries of Man's soul, even as all Thinkers, in all ages, have devoutly read it there: that Time and space are not God, but creations of God; that with God as it is a universal Here, so it is an everlasting Now.

And again:

Was Luther's Picture of the Devil less a Reality, whether it were formed within the bodily eye, or without it? In every the wisest Soul lies a whole world of internal Madness, an authentic Demon-Empire; out of which, indeed, his world of Wisdom has been creatively built together, and now rests there, as on its dark foundations does a habitable flowery Earth-rind.

Keats's belief is quite as thorough-going as Carlyle's. So far from depending upon the sensuous world about him for mental food and spiritual substance, he asserts in effect that the poet's power rests largely on a subjective basis, upon his ability to create from the materials of his own brain, his intellect operating upon things of the visible world, in close relation with ideal truth and beauty, a new spiritual reality that embraces and comprehends both the known and the unknown verities, like, yet unlike, each — ethereal substance " greater even than our Creator himself has made." Of this the world of environment need furnish but a fractional part; yet, let us remember how vital a part it is. The world we see is entirely real, and, though it is but a small portion of a much larger unseen whole, a thorough knowledge of it is necessary to an understanding of the ideal entity to whose inner workings it gives the clue.

Such is the power of creative imagination, a seeing, reconciling, combining force that seizes the old, penetrates beneath its surface, disengages the truth lying slumbering there, and, building afresh, bodies forth anew a reconstructed universe in fair forms of artistic power and beauty.

CHAPTER VIII

WHAT IS BEAUTY?

I

"Beauty is truth, truth beauty," — that is all
Ye know on earth, and all ye need to know.

"To see things in their beauty," writes Matthew Arnold
rather enigmatically of this passage, " is to see things in their
truth, and Keats knew it." One wishes the great critic had
gone on to explain what Keats means by seeing "things in
their beauty." To know that would be to hold the key to
Keats's aesthetic philosophy. For it was the yearning passion
for the beautiful that held the young poet steadily to his
course. " I feel assured I should write from the mere yearning and fondness I have for the beautiful," he once declared
to Richard Woodhouse, in a moment of warm confidence,
" even if my night's labours should be burnt every Morning,
and no eye ever shine upon them." He looked to this passion
as the infallible sign of his fellowship with the poetic genius
of all time; it was to him the way to vision, power, and truth.
" If I should die," he wrote to Fanny Brawne, as he lay sick
shortly before his death, " I have left no immortal work behind me — nothing to make my friends proud of my memory
— but I have lov'd the principle of beauty in all things, and
if I had had time I would have made myself remember'd."
Beauty, with Keats, was not only the open sesame to poetic
life and truth, it was truth itself: "What the Imagination
seizes as Beauty must be Truth, whether it existed before or
not." As we have seen in the last chapter, the method of the
imagination as opposed to reasoning and the scientific approach is that of emotionalized intuitive perception. A sense
of spiritual reality which the mind apprehends imaginatively,

then, or immediately rather than indirectly, is Beauty; this is also Truth. When Keats refers to Beauty in this sense, so far from limiting himself to mere sensuous beauty, he is speaking of something entirely outside the realm of the sensuous, except as physical objects may be its expression; he means enduring universal truth — the Idea as it were.

The view that this beauty might be not only perceived, but even created by the imagination, Keats held to the end, but with conditional modifications. He believed in it just as earnestly in March, 1819, when he declared, " Beauty is truth, truth beauty," as when he asserted his faith in the powers of imagination to seize or even create beauty, in 1817, but long before that he had learned to qualify specifically that the imagination should be trained and disciplined by close contact with the world of men. He had discovered through experience the wide gap between the futile soaring of uneducated Fancy into this dream world, and the sober flights of an imagination loaded with the stored-up wisdom of life. The first ends in a vision of mawkish unreality, the second in revelations of high truth. So in later years, Keats would have said, " What the wise Imagination seizes as Beauty must be Truth." In other words Beauty is truth arrived at through the intuitive perception of an intellectualized imagination — an imagination weighted with experience, with thought, with judgment.

With reference to a work of art, Beauty is the emotional recognition of the life-truth revealed there. Indeed, this beauty is the very essence of truth, for it is truth unclouded by such extrinsic considerations as time or place or moral relationships; it is truth subjective and emancipated; it is truth eternal, an immortal verity of the everlasting universe.

I can best show what I mean by turning to the evidence Keats himself has left us as to his conception of Beauty.

When the German critic Wincklemann first came into contact with Greek art his interest at once centered in form. That which attracted him most as characteristic in the work of Phidias, Praxiteles, and the rest was a harmony of proportion, graceful lines, and pleasing contours. To him physical loveliness was of primary, expression, of secondary, importance. Hence, Wincklemann based his critique of Greek art largely on beauty of form. But when Keats became acquainted with Greek sculpture, if we are to judge from the testimony that comes down to us, loveliness of form seems to have made little appeal to him. It rather seems that in the presence of the Elgin Marbles his whole being was flooded with the light of life that flashed into his soul through the medium of the sculptured figures before him. It is worth noting that in the two sonnets on the Elgin Marbles, the most direct expression of this great artistic experience, there is scarcely a reference to fair form or sensuous beauty. On the contrary, we see that the young Keats had been numbed, awed, almost overpowered by the mighty vision of life and truth revealed to him. In the first he offers an apology to Haydon for his inability to express his real appreciation of the sculpture, and praises Haydon for his part in securing national recognition of their worth. I quote it here:

> Haydon! forgive me that I cannot speak
>   Definitively of these mighty things;
> Forgive me, that I have not eagle's wings,
> That what I want I know not where to seek.
> And think that I would not be over-meek,
>   In rolling out upfollow'd thunderings,
>   Even to the steep of Heliconian springs,
> Were I of ample strength for such a freak.
> Think, too, that all these numbers should be thine;
> Whose else? In this who touch thy vesture's hem?
> For, when men stared at what was most divine
> With brainless idiotism and o'erwise phlegm
> Thou hadst beheld the full Hesperian shrine
> Of their star in the east, and gone to worship them! [1]

[1] Written the last of February or early in March, 1817. Haydon was from the first an ardent champion of the Elgin Marbles, and maintained, in the face of the most heated opposition, their validity and genuineness as true works of the Phidian school. He talked and wrote until his arguments finally prevailed and the public accepted the sculpture at its real value. Haydon had introduced Keats to the marbles at the British Museum early in March, 1819.

The second sonnet gives the better idea of the sensations the poet felt as he stood in the presence of the marbles and drank in their beauty:

> My spirit is too weak; mortality
> Weighs heavily on me like unwilling sleep,
> And each imagined pinnacle and steep
> Of godlike hardship tells me I must die
> Like a sick eagle looking at the sky.
>   Yet 'tis a gentle luxury to weep,
> That I have not the cloudy wings to keep
> Fresh for the opening of the morning's eye.
> Such dim-conceived glories of the brain
>   Bring round the heart an indescribable feud;
> So do these wonders a most dizzy pain,
>   That mingles Grecian grandeur with the rude
> Wasting of old Time — with a billowy main
> A sun, a shadow of a magnitude.

What do we learn from these sonnets? Simply that the marbles have set the young poet's imagination all afire. The impressions are vague and confused, partly because of the vastness of the images that come thronging into his brain, partly because in the presence of true art, he realizes with a sort of sick terror how far distant for him is the goal of success in poetry. But it is evident that the mere surface beauty, the appearance, of the marbles is not primarily what moves him; he is concerned with their deeper significance, their emotional appeal, the truth they portray.

Crowding his excited brain are dimly-conceived visions of the whole cycle of human progress, the rise and fall of civilizations, the meaning of man and the world. There is here in the splendid last lines almost a perfect expression of a momentary glimpse of infinitude, the sublime infinitude of eternity — a fluttering, elusive mental grasp of the vast and incomprehensible universe — " Grecian grandeur " mingled with the " rude

> Wasting of old Time — with a billowy main
> A sun, a shadow of a magnitude.

It is a partial re-echo of that overwhelming sense of wonder and awe Keats experienced in first reading Chapman's *Homer*, so admirably conveyed in the description of Cortez and his men who stared at the Pacific, then

> Look'd at each other with a wild surmise —
> Silent, upon a peak in Darien.

It is also another instance of Keats's rare gift for unusually vivid expression of the sense of vastness and mystery, two of the best additional examples occurring, one at the end of his sonnet, *When I Have Fears That I May Cease to Be* —

> . . . then on the shore
> Of the wide world I stand alone, and think,
> Till Love and Fame to nothingness do sink. —

and one in *Endymion* Book II, lines 160–163:

> . . . But for me,
> There is no depth to strike in: I can see
> Nought earthly worth my compassing; so stand
> Upon a misty, jutting head of land —
> Alone.

So it is evident from this sonnet, not one of his best, but one of his most serious, that to Keats the beauty of the marbles consists in their capacity to set the imagination into such play as to arouse anew in the spectator the vision of life the artist had originally caught and then portrayed in the plastic figures upon which he worked. This for the observer is the moment of arrival at " that trembling delicate and snail-horn perception of beauty," of which Keats writes elsewhere — the moment of realization of the identity of form with content, of beauty with truth. It is the instant of the completed fabric of the creative imagination, either for the artist or for him who understands his art. That is, in looking upon a Grecian urn the creative imagination of the observer arrives at the same point as did the creative imagination of the artist — a delicate, snail-horn perception of the truth — the Idea — expressed in the urn; hence the beauty of it. The mere external aspects of an urn would not make it beautiful, a thing of art, to Keats. It is rather that the symbols executed there, themselves a product of mind and soul, still contain within themselves a dynamic something, itself the offspring of imaginative insight, that has the power to set aflame the mind and soul of an imaginative observer: that is true art, that, beauty; that is truth preserved in enduring form for the ages. " For soul is form and doth the body make."

To this add the evidence contained in one of Keats's letters to his brother and sister-in-law concerning his enjoyment and understanding of Raphael and others.

> I never can feel certain of any truth, but from a clear perception of its Beauty — and I find myself very young-minded even in that perceptive power — which I hope will increase. A year ago, I could not understand in the slightest degree Raphael's Cartoons — now I begin to read them a little. And how did I learn to do so? By seeing something done in quite an opposite spirit — I mean a picture of Guido's in which all the Saints, instead of that heroic simplicity and unaffected grandeur which they inherit from Raphael, had each of them both in countenance and gesture all the canting, solemn, melodramatic mawkishness of Mackenzie's Father Nicholas. When I was last at Haydon's I looked over a Book of Prints taken from the fresco of the Church of Milan, the name of which I forget — in it are comprised Specimens of the first and second age of Art in Italy. I do not think I ever had a greater treat out of Shakespeare. Full of romance and the most tender feeling — magnificence of draperies beyond everything I ever saw, not excepting Raphael's. But Grotesque to a curious pitch — yet still making up a fine whole — even finer to me than more accomplish'd works — as there was left so much room for Imagination. [2]

Again the emphasis is not upon lines and colors, but upon the meaning of the cartoons, as compared with the empty superficiality of the Mackenzie picture. How does one get a perception of meaning from a work of art? The Milan Prints are even finer than many more accomplished works, for example, the Raphaels, for the reason that more is left to the

[2] *To George and Georgiana Keats.* Dec., 1818. Forman. Vol. IV, page 202.

imagination. Evidently, it is through the kindling of the imagination into a flame of intuitive perceptive activity that the beauty — the truth — of any work of art is revealed. There is only one suggestion of sensuous beauty — the " magnificence of draperies " — but the emphasis is not on this.

In December, 1817, Keats had the privilege of visiting the private art gallery of Mr. West,[3] then President of the Royal Academy.[4] He records his impressions in his usual direct and acute manner:[5]

I spent Friday evening with Wells,[6] and went next morning to see " Death on a Pale Horse." It is a wonderful picture, when West's age is considered; but there is nothing to be intense upon, no woman one feels mad to kiss, no face swelling into reality. The excellence of every art is its intensity, capable of making all disagreeables evaporate from their being in close relationship with Beauty and Truth. Examine " King Lear," and you will find this exemplified throughout; but in this picture we have unpleasantness without any momentous depth of speculation excited, in which to bury its repulsiveness.

The " no woman one feels mad to kiss " and " no face swelling into reality " almost sounds like a sensuous man talking, but the rest of the comment is redemptive, making clear that Keats demanded of a work of art such an intensity of imaginative effect that figures in it should take their place in their proper settings in real life, with enough dynamic suggestiveness to send the onlooker into a state of imaginative speculation upon life itself and his relation to it. Certainly it is this " momentous depth of speculation" that is of paramount concern.

[3] W. T. Young in his introduction to Keats's *Endymion and Other Poems* points out how large an influence painters and lovers and students of art exerted in Keats's life. He names several of these, most of whom were his closest friends — Hunt, art collector; Hazlitt, painter and critic; Severn, painter; Haydon, painter; Lamb, student and critic of art. (Pp. XX–XXI.)

[4] This gallery is described by Hunt in his Autobiography, Vol. I, pp. 100–103.

[5] *To George and Thomas Keats.* Dec., 1817. Forman. Vol. IV, p. 49.

[6] Charles Wells, the author of *Stories After Nature* and *Joseph and His Brethren.*

Keats mentions *King Lear* as an example of a thing done in
the contrary spirit. Here is intensity in " such close relationship with Beauty and Truth " that all disagreeables evaporate
in contemplating the work. On January 23, 1818, Keats sat
down to read *King Lear* again and wrote the sonnet, now so
well known, expressing the feeling and speculations that the
great tragedy inspired in him:

> O Golden-Tongued Romance with serene lute!
> Fair plumed Syren! Queen of far away!
> Leave melodizing on this wintry day,
> Shut up thine olden pages, and be mute:
> Adieu! for once again the fierce dispute,
> Betwixt damnation and impassion'd clay
> Must I burn through; once more humbly assay
> The bitter-sweet of this Shakespearian fruit.
> Chief Poet! and ye clouds of Albion,
> Begetters of our deep eternal theme,
> When through the old oak forest I am gone,
> Let me not wander in a barren dream,
> But when I am consumed in the fire,
> Give me new Phoenix wings to fly at my desire.

What is this fierce dispute

> Betwixt damnation and impassion'd clay

but a picture of life itself projected in such intensity of reality
that disagreeables vanish and end in an imaginative grasp of
truth and beauty?[7] This is a beauty that far transcends sensuous loveliness; it is rooted in an intuitive knowledge of the
human heart and the spiritual laws of life.

Then let us turn to the *Ode on a Grecian Urn* itself. One
keen reading with an eye to the sonnets on the Elgin Marbles,
is sufficient to show that what has stirred the heart of the poet
is the imaginative picture of Greek life in its relation to all
existence represented here. Let us look for a moment at what
Keats sees in the various pieces of art that formed the inspira-

---

[7] This could apply only to tragedy and serious epic. But when Keats
talked of the highest poetry he always meant these.

tion for this poem. What he really does in the ode is to describe a series of pictures or scenes that he imagines must have formed the basis for the artists' work, and to give us his own speculations growing out of his contemplation of the sculptured representation of these scenes. The external aspects of the urn do not constitute its beauty. It is rather that the symbols executed here, themselves a product of mind and soul, still contain within themselves a dynamic something that has power to kindle the imagination of a sympathetic observer, who not only is able to re-create the particular bit of life that furnished the material through which the artist worked, but can also catch the gleam beyond, the vision of the universal that the creator of the piece himself conceived. This is what Keats saw in the urn, and in this is its beauty.

The urn for Keats is a transparent glass, a powerful lens, through which there stands revealed a miniature pageant of the past merging into the present of all time; here is a portrayal of a tiny portion of the verities of the ages which it is art's business to perceive, interpret, and preserve. This comes to the mind of Keats in a pleasurable wave of recognition. It is pleasurable because he detects, starting out at him from the fair chiselled form, waves of intuitive whisperings that seize his imagination and set it all aflame; it is pleasurable, moreover, because in the intensity of speculation that follows, there comes a sense of discovery of truth; and it is not mere fact or logical conclusion he perceives, nor is it a moral precept, nor a religious idea; it is rather like a revelation of a principle of existence, a perception of a law of life, an insight into the universal human heart. So to Keats truth arrived at through emotionalized imaginative perception is beauty, and beauty is truth.

This is a conception of Beauty wide enough to include in its scope representations of the ugly and tragic, as well as the fair and pleasant things of life. We have already seen in our study of Keats's attempts to reconcile his dream world with the actual that he had found in the detached contemplative state a means to a pleasurable attitude toward even the harsh cruelty of nature and the false and mean activities of men — because there was something fine in the energies displayed, in themselves. Therefore, all ended, not in revulsion, but in speculation. In the extracts I have given in this chapter, there are passages that reveal flashes of rarest insight into the whole problem of the ugly in art. One of these, " The excellence of every art is its intensity, capable of making all disagreeables evaporate from their being in close relationship with Beauty and Truth," is, as Sidney Colvin declares, "a sentence worth whole treatises, and fit, sketchy as it is, to serve as text to all that can justly be discoursed concerning problems of art in its relation to nature, — of realism, romance, and the rest." (*John Keats*, page 253.) Perhaps this is praise a trifle extravagant, but certainly we have here an admirable beginning for a dissertation on the aesthetics of the painful and the ugly. We may conclude from the tenor of the passage in which Keats makes this observation that there was no beauty in Mr. West's *Death on a Pale Horse*. Why? Because there was nothing intense enough to grip the imagination and raise it from the lowlands of the particular commonplace and sordid to the heights of free speculation upon the universal. On the contrary, the prints of Milanese frescoes, many of them " grotesque to a certain degree," contain more beauty than many a finer work — "they leave more to the imagination"; in other words, give rise to images the mind may be intense upon, and so excite more vivid perceptions of the real and true.

King Lear exemplifies the capacity of a work of art wrought from the materials of pain and folly to produce that detached speculative state of spirit essential to a memorable aesthetic experience. This is brought about through an intensity sufficient to stir the imagination to a " momentous depth of speculation." How admirably do Keats's words describe the adventure! The phrase " burn through " depicts the nature and the intensity of the imaginative re-creative revelation; and " fierce dispute betwixt damnation and impassion'd clay" are words that reveal in themselves without help from other lines how far Keats's mind is projected on its way in speculation by this vivid representation of tragic reality, all portrayed with such intensity that disagreeables vanish and end in an imaginative grasp of truth and beauty.

Here in brief, seems to be Keats's theory as to the possibility of creating beauty out of the ugly and evil: Take any subject, however repulsive, and represent it in an art form with enough vigorous universal life-truth gleaming through to excite intense imaginative speculation and insight, and the unpleasantness vanishes — is not recognized; what one sees is a vision of life, and there comes an elevation of soul that carries one for the moment away from the accidents of time and place. But that gleam of vitalized truth lacking, a repulsive object represented in art is — repulsive and ugly. It is a simple creed, yet, as Colvin says, in its naked statement one worth whole treatises on art. It is entirely and admirably consistent with Keats's large theory that a direct and intuitive perception of truth is Beauty.

II

Hyperion was undoubtedly planned by Keats as his greatest poem. He had looked ahead to it while he was still writing *Endymion;* he consecrated himself for his great task by a year of study and reflection; that he might be better fitted for it he plunged again into Milton and strove to understand his mighty genius, travelled into Scotland on a toilsome walking tour in order to load his imagination with grander scenes and mountains, and strengthened his intellect by the most arduous thought on the great problems of art and life. " Throughout twelve months of strenuous intellectual effort," declares Mr. de Selincourt in his Warton Lecture, " *Hyperion* was seldom from his mind." Even more than the *Endymion,* the *Hyperion* was to be a supreme test of his powers. What was to be its theme? Milton had sung in his masterpiece of the fall of man and the plan for his redemption; his setting had been heaven and hell and all that lies between; his personages, the angels and archangels of the spheres. Dante had traced the progress of a soul through the mysteries of the unknown other-worlds. Could Keats, who hopefully planned to be "among the English poets after death," choose a less lofty subject in marking out the limits of his supreme work? As one would expect, he did not. His original plan was an epic on a large scale, probably not less than ten books long. The characters were to be the Titan gods of the infant world and the Olympian powers who overthrew them; its setting was to be the earth, the air, and the far-flung spaces of the revolving sun. The theme is the triumph of Beauty, the progress of the human intellect, the evolution of man's mind from trust in brute force and the imperfect knowledge of mere reason to the god-like wisdom of intuitive understanding. Shelley had been writing a large-scale dramatic poem representing the emancipation of the mind of man from its age-long errors and superstitions. It is not probable that Keats was influenced by this, or even knew of it, but his conception is akin to Shelley's evolutionary idea as a step in the general progress of man's mind toward a higher level. But we must believe that Keats is here portraying the last highest stage in human mental progress — the stage where the imaginative wisdom of man matches empyrean vision and reality.

It was as natural for Keats to turn to Greek mythology for the setting and figures for his epic as for Milton to go to the Bible and theology for his *Paradise Lost,* and for a parallel in evolution it would be impossible to find metal more attractive than the Greek myths of successive creations.[8] The evolutionary conception emerges in the speech of Oceanus in which he points out that the Titan dynasty has fallen " by course of natural law." To Saturn he explains,

[8] Though it is probable that the Greeks themselves had no notion whatever of evolution. " The notion of a world evolution was wholly alien to the Greeks," says Bosanquet in his *History of Aesthetics,* p. 325.

> And first, as thou wast not the first of powers,
> So art thou not the last; it cannot be:
> Thou art not the beginning nor the end.
>
> (*Hyperion*, Book II, ll. 188–190.)

For just as light succeeded chaos and "parental darkness,"
and touched "the whole enormous matter into life" and
form; just

> As Heaven and Earth are fairer, fairer far
> Than Chaos and blank Darkness,

so it is with the gods, since

> . . . on our heels a fresh perfection treads
> A power more strong in beauty.

Against this fate it is vain to murmur or complain. To do so
is as idle as for the dull earth to " quarrel with the proud
forests " that have sprung from it,

> . . . for 'tis the eternal law
> That first in beauty should be first in might.

Here is evolution, upward evolution. *Hyperion*, as Mr. Ker
says, in his essay in the *John Keats Memorial Volume*, " was
a poem of progress "; moreover, it is a poem of steady, certain
progress. Keats had before talked of the gregarious march
of the human intellect.[9] Now he gives some idea as to the
nature of that march and its destination.

The questions raised as we read *Hyperion* are, What does
this new race possess that is denied the Titans? What is this
beauty in which lies their strength? Was it that the individuals of the old dispensation were lacking in the glorious re-
splendent physical beauty due to gods? Hardly: it is a frequent comment among critics that *Hyperion* was given up
because Keats had made the Hyperion order so dazzling that
it would be hopeless to attempt to create beings to surpass

[9] In the Mansion of Life letter. Mr. Ker mentions this too, but he does
not suggest toward what the intellect is marching.

them. It is not even that these gods did not possess some of the gentler virtues. Saturn mourns —

> . . . and I am smother'd up,
> And buried from all godlike exercise
> Of influence benign on planets pale,
> Of admonitions to the wind and seas,
> Of peaceful sway above man's harvesting,
> And all those acts which Deity supreme
> Doth ease his heart of love in.
>
> (Book I, ll. 106–113.)

Benignity, even love, Saturn has shown, in his rule of the earth and the planets. And he has been powerful. He and his kind have created and fashioned a universe. He could do it again, he feels. And Hyperion! Brilliant, regal Hyperion, blazing in glory and fortified in his splendid palace of light, why must he fall?

To be concise, I think Hyperion and the rest went down just as incomplete and imperfect knowledge, largely dependent on reason, must ever give way to complete and perfect knowledge with its origin largely in direct imaginative perception. Hyperion fell before a power " more strong in Beauty," more strong, that is, in ability to understand and grasp and use the secrets of the universe, more strong in soul knowledge, as it were.

We have seen that there are two qualities that Keats held to belong to perfect knowledge: first, to comprehend completely through disciplined imagination; second, to have reached a state in mental stature where all facts, pleasant or otherwise, will appear in their proper perspective as subjects for contemplation, and not as materials to excite the fears and passions. The ideal is nowhere better expressed than when in *Hyperion*, Oceanus, Keats's own oracle in this poem, declares:

> Now comes the pain of truth, to whom 'tis pain;
> O folly! for to bear all naked truths,
> And to envisage circumstance, all calm,
> That is the top of sovereignty.
>
> (Book II, ll. 202–205.)

But the Saturn-Hyperion dynasty possesses neither of these elements. Oceanus comes near to both; it is somewhat of a defect in the consistency of the piece for him to have been able to find the avenue —

> Through which I wandered to eternal truth,

and to have in his face

> . . . that severe content
> Which comes from thought and musing.

But perhaps he is just " a little lower than the angels." He can perceive, but cannot apply his wisdom. Gentle, poetic Clymene stands next in intuitive perception and calm. Just as Oceanus has come to an understanding of the laws of evolution and of the necessity for powers of less perfection to succumb to those of greater beauty, so she has detected something of the secret of that new beauty in the music of Apollo and knows that there is no hope of reinstatement. But as for the rest, there seems no trace of knowledge or of calm. Old Saturn searches his stock of lore and pores over " Nature's universal scroll " all to no purpose; he cannot understand the mystery of his humiliating fall. Then he gives himself up to vain passions, and we behold the sad spectacle of

> . . . the supreme God
> At war with all the frailty of grief,
> Of rage, of fear, anxiety, revenge,
> Remorse, spleen, hope, but most of all despair.
>
> (Book I, ll. 92–95.)

And so with the others. Keats's description of the scene is a masterpiece in its delineation of the rage and despair of frustrated ambition. Enceladus is plotting, " tiger-passion'd " and " lion-thought'd "; a " shattered rib of rock " testifies to the rage of Creus; Iapetus savagely squeezes with clenched fingers the neck of a serpent, until its barbed tongue protrudes; and others show their pain and anger in various horrid ways. As for Hyperion, he storms about the palace of the sun all " full of wrath " and fear and foreboding.

Now this is all ungodlike, as Cœlus, whispering to Hyperion, makes plain. In fact, it is in this likeness to mere mortals in their inability to know and comprehend in serene strength and repose that the weakness of these gods seems to lie. Cœlus has seen Saturn fall and fears Hyperion is near the same doom:

> For I have seen my sons most unlike Gods.
> Divine ye were created, and divine
> In sad demeanor, solemn, undisturb'd,
> Unruffled, like high Gods, ye liv'd and ruled:
> Now I behold in you fear, hope, and wrath;
> Actions of rage and passion; even as
> I see them, on the mortal world beneath,
> In men who die. — This is the grief, O Son!
> Sad sign of ruin, sudden dismay, and fall!
>
> (Book I, ll. 327–336.)

This " fear, hope, and wrath " of the Titans grows from a baffling sense of inferiority, a consciousness that greater powers " more strong in beauty " have appeared and that for them the sun has set — even as ambitious men rage without, but tremble within when superiors threaten their domain.

In the meantime what of Apollo? In the island of Delos he is wandering about, uncomforted. Even the consciousness of his perfect accomplishment wrought from the lyre, of which Mnemosyne speaks —

> Whose strings touch'd by thy fingers, all the vast
> Unwearied ear of the whole universe
> Listen'd in pain and pleasure —
>
> (Book III, ll. 64–66.)

gives him no joy. He is restless, weeping, utterly unhappy. He craves knowledge, not ordinary knowledge, but a wide all-embracing understanding. " Painful, vile oblivion " seals his eyes, and his frantic soul strains to burst the barriers that veil the mysteries from his sight.

What are the stars?   There is the sun, the sun!

.   .   .   .

> . . . Where is power?
> Whose hand, whose essence, what divinity
> Makes this alarum in the elements,
> While I here idle listen on the shores
> In fearless yet in aching ignorance?
>
> (Book III, ll. 97–107.)

He must know the secrets of existence, its creator, and his purpose.

And then the miracle happens. The intense longing to know is father of the realization. Mnemosyne does not speak; nevertheless, Apollo learns all. In one mighty wave of revelation supreme truth flashes itself into the soul of this young god — the representative of a new order of love and beauty and wisdom on earth.

> Knowledge enormous makes a God of me,

he cries.

But it is intuitive knowledge, gained neither by book, nor precept, nor consecutive reasoning, that he now possesses. And it is this, linked with his already sweet gift of song, that is to give Apollo the power, the strength, and the perfection to enable him to dispossess the comparatively crass Hyperion.

With Apollo the moment of deification through knowledge is the moment of the birth of Beauty in his soul. It is not an easy birth, but is accomplished in a travail of agony that is "like the struggle at the gate of death": Keats wanted to show that only those could attain the heights of insight who had known suffering and misery.

It is through this transcendent gift of Beauty that Apollo was to dethrone the apparently incomparable Hyperion. For proof that the other Titans had been displaced by the same power, we may rely upon the testimony of the oracle Oceanus. Of his own successor, he says:

> Have ye beheld the young God of the Seas,
> My dispossessor? Have ye seen his face?
>
> .   .   .   .
>
> I saw him on the calmed waters scud,
> With such a glow of beauty in his eyes,
> That it enforc'd me to bid sad farewell
> To all my empire.
>
> (Book II, ll. 232–239.)

The " glow of beauty in his eyes " is the light from that higher knowledge that is to take possession of the earth in the new evolutionary order. Had Keats gone on with the poem, there would have been presented the spectacle of the deposition of the blazing, effulgent sun-god, not by one more brilliant in physical beauty but by one with understanding and glorious god-like knowledge.

And so we come back to our definition of Beauty as a subjective conception of truth reached through imaginative perception. I cannot agree with Mr. Bradley, in his *Keats and "Philosophy,"* that while the two are for Keats the same, they are yet " reached, apprehended, and expressed " in different ways. I believe that Keats knew only one way to the deepest truths of life and the highest realities of the realms that lie beyond consciousness of this and the super-world, and that was through the power of the penetrative imagination — the soul of man reaching out to the great all-soul. There is, however, always this qualification: the soul that is to see far must have its lessons; it cannot be that of a mere dreamer, it cannot be one of those contented beings, who, no matter how wise and good, no matter how much they love their fellows and, " like slaves to poor humanity, labor for mortal good," still

> . . . seek no wonder but the human face,
> No music but a happy-noted voice.
> (*The Fall of Hyperion,* Canto I, ll. 163–164.)

It must rather be that of a dreamer who strives to see beyond the limits of earthly things into the vast empyrean mists, and

yet knows well the " giant agony of the world," knows, in fact,
that it is only through the discipline of this world of misery
that the imagination can be strengthened for the higher flights.

That is one thing Keats tried to make very plain in *The
Fall of Hyperion*. He had failed to do this in the early version. He had meant to show that Apollo received his gift of
divine knowledge through agony and suffering, had intended
to prove that this experience was necessary to his transforma-
tion. But neither the fierce convulsions that shook him as he
was born into his new life, nor all his anguish and shrieks
were convincing. Keats recognized this. He had in *Endymion*
failed to convey his idea to the public, had realized it and
suffered for it. He had now grown more fastidious in the
matter of clearness, and was not content to go on in a course
that meant a repetition of his former failure. So he aban-
dons the poem, right at the point where its obscurity is most
manifest, and then tries again. In *The Fall of Hyperion,* he
leaves no room for doubt. The ground is cleared in the first
third of the first book, and no one can now fail to see that
the highest beauty can be perceived only by those who know
life in its deepest aspects. In fact, in order to show that the
mere visionary cannot succeed, Keats goes so far that he
is likely to be misunderstood as condemning the " dreamer
tribe " altogether; but the facts are he does find a place of
honor for the true dreamer who can also tell his dreams:

> For Poesy alone can tell her dreams, —
> With the fine spell of words alone can save
> Imagination from the sable chain
> And dumb enchantment. (*The Fall of Hyperion.*
> Canto I, ll. 8–11.)

Decisively, Keats teaches in this book, however, that empty
dreams won't do. Mr. Bradley says that with Keats " Beauty
is reached through sense and imagination, truth in or by
' thought,' ' knowledge,' or ' philosophy.' " But no; Keats
could not come to any real Truth, not the kind he talks of

here, through " thought " or through " philosophy." " I can never be certain of a Truth except through a clear conception of its Beauty " — its imaginative reality, — he declares; and, again, " I cannot see how one can arrive at truth through consecutive reasoning." No, for Keats even the road to Truth [10] and Beauty are the same. Thought, knowledge, and philosophy are, as we have seen, essential components to clear intuitive seeing, but they are components only. They are often ends of the seeing process, but they are never the uncompounded agents. Only an educated, seer-like imagination, ballasted by the wisdom of the earth, can wing its way with steady sureness to the heart of the " Mystery." To possess such an imagination is to be strong in a beauty that shall some day rule the earth. It was this power that enabled the Olympians to upset the Titan dynasty, and by virtue of its perfect fruition Apollo was to cast the sun-god from his throne.

III

From what has preceded, it is not difficult to deduce an explanation for that other famed line, " A thing of beauty is a joy forever." True pleasure, true joy and happiness, consist in being able to perceive eternal beauty. What is beautiful, that is, what is true, in any one age remains so for all ages; therefore, what gives the highest joy remains ever the same. Ruskin, condemning the line as untrue, declares it should read, " A thing of beauty is a law forever." The chances are that Keats understood what he was saying much more fully than Ruskin, yet perhaps might have written *law* rather than *joy* with equal truth. For with Keats, a thing of beauty is a discovered law of life, an eternal principle of the universe.

The permanence of beauty does not depend upon the life and death of any one individual; its agent is the individual, but its existence transcends the cycles of generations through

[10] I speak here of permanent, universal truth, not of the particular facts and the reasoned conclusions of everyday life.

which it reveals itself. The essence of beauty endures all ravages of time.

> Thou wast not born for death, immortal Bird!
> No hungry generations tread thee down;
> The voice I hear this passing night was heard
> In ancient days by emperor and clown:
> Perhaps the self-same song that found a path
> Through the sad heart of Ruth, when, sick for home,
> She stood in tears amid the alien corn;
> The same that oft-times hath
> Charm'd magic casements, opening on the foam
> Of perilous seas, in faery lands forlorn.
>
> (*Ode to a Nightingale,* VII.)

Of this stanza, Mr. J. M. Robertson, in his *New Essays Toward a Critical Method,* says, "It must be confessed — even Mr. Forman allows it — that the logic of the stanza is wrong; and it will scarcely do to argue, as Mr. Forman does in regard to the first stanza, that the obscurity is appropriate." But, on the contrary, is not the logic secure? Is not the beauty of the nightingale's song immortal? Is not the fairness of Sheba the same deathless loveliness of entrancing women of all ages? Has not the sweetness of the rose that quickens your glad pulses today the same ineffable enchantment that softened the hearts of Indian princes in ages gone? Is not Keats here saying anew, " A thing of beauty is a joy forever "? The mere temporal agent for that beauty — the feathered songster, the garden bush, the human body — may decay, but the beauty, the essence of being, the truth, the idea, cannot die; it is eternal.[11] The sensuous real present here recalls the ideal eternal, and in imagination the poet feels the melodious

---

[11] Compare Hegel's remarks on the same subject:

"Upon that which, in works of art, the mind borrows from its own inner life, it is able, even on the side of external existence, to confer permanence; whereas the individual living thing of nature is transient, vanishing and mutable in its aspect, while the work of art persists. Though, indeed, it is not mere permanence, but the accentuation of the character which animation by mind confers, that constitutes its genuine preëminence as compared with natural reality." — *Philosophy of Fine Art.*

notes of the beautiful singer near him stirring the hearts of men of all ages — and so for him this beauty " is a joy forever " — as all true beauty must be.

In the *Ode on a Grecian Urn* art in its enduring permanence is compared with brief and fleeting human life, and there is quite as clear an implication as to the eternity of the Truth and Beauty which the artist has captured and fixed in his medium of relatively temporary art form. The permanence of the unheard melodies, the love, the beauty, is greater than the life of a mere work of art. Grecian urns of whatever beauty shall crumble away, but the human passions, the universal truths represented there, shall endure. An echo of the idea of immortal beauty found in the *Ode to a Nightingale* occurs in the lines,

> And happy melodist, unwearied,
> Forever piping songs forever new,

and an evidence of Keats's conception of the content of the nightingale's song is found in these lines from *Bards of Passion and of Mirth:*

> Where the nightingale doth sing
> Not a senseless, tranced thing,
> But divine melodious truth;
> Philosophic numbers smooth;
> Tales and golden histories
> Of heaven and its mysteries.

These songs shall surely go on long after the most solid marble has slivered into atoms.

Wherein does this permanent beauty have its being? What is the nature of the universe in which it resides? There are times when one finds in Keats strong leanings toward Platonic conceptions, others when we think of him as Hegelian in his thinking. Platonic and Hegelian he seems in turn, though perhaps in truth his thought is that of neither, but something all his own.

Sir Sidney Colvin, Professor Bradley, and others have noted

the Platonic strain, but have dismissed the idea of Plato's influence as improbable. "He had read no Plato," says Colvin, " though he was of course familiar enough with Spenser's mellifluous dilution of Platonic and neo-Platonic doctrine in his four *Hymns*.' And Mr. Bradley declares, "He uses the name of Plato for a rhyme in a jocular poem, but there is no sign that he had read a word of Plato or knew that he had written of beauty as well as truth."

But these gentlemen are overlooking certain facts. Consider the schoolmasters of Keats — his circle of friends and those whose writings he followed closely. There was Hunt. Now Hunt was not a university man, but he was intimate with those who were, Shelley for instance; Shelley knew his Plato thoroughly. And Hunt was quite cognizant of this fact. He speaks of Shelley's daily reading at Marlow as consisting of " Plato, or Homer, one of the Greek tragedians, or the Bible "; [12] and in connection with Shelley's loss of his children at the hands of the government for his opinions, Hunt mentions other famous men who, like Shelley, would have been deprived of their children on account of their writings: " The virtuous Condorcet, if he had been an Englishman and a father would have stood no chance. Plato, for his Republic, would have stood as little." [13] It is needless to speak of the large circle of Hunt's other literary friends, who of course had read Plato — Lamb, Hazlitt, and Coleridge, for example. So, undoubtedly, Hunt was himself versed in Platonic doctrine, even though he had read no Plato personally, which was unlikely. In his *Essays* he writes of " The greatest of all poets (who, according to Plato, is God)." [14] And again he says: " Whether we think the sun is a substance, or only the image of a divine thought, an idea, a thing imaginary, we are equally agreed as to the notion of its warmth." [15] The point to this is that if Leigh Hunt knew Plato, Keats must have understood him quite as well; they were long the most intimate of com-

[12] *Lord Byron and Some of His Contemporaries.* I. 323.
[13] *Ibid.*, p. 320. [14] *On the Borders of Poetry*, p. 1.
[15] *On Realities of the Imagination,* in *Essays,* p. 67.

panions. Then there was Benjamin Bailey, the Oxford student and rector, one of Keats's closest friends. In the summer
of 1817, Keats spent five or six weeks with Benjamin Bailey
at Oxford.[16] Keats was writing *Endymion*, Bailey was studying. Every day they took a walk and talked about everything. It is hardly possible that in these walks this young
Oxford scholar would fail to discuss Plato and the other philosophers he must have been reading. I need not mention the
possible influence of Cowden Clark, scholar and son of a
scholar, of Haydon, of Reynolds, Severn, and Lamb — all of
whom were unquestionably familiar with the Platonic doctrines; most of them, certainly through Coleridge, understood
something of Kant, Herder, Fichte, and Schelling. May it
not be supposed then that Keats was fairly familiar with
Plato and even with other philosophic ideas current in his day
— second hand perhaps; but an idea is quite as real received
by word of mouth as through the printed page. Curious that
we so often forget this fact. Jesus wrote no word, neither did
Socrates.

At any rate, here and there we get a distinct Platonic in-
tonation. Thus in *Hyperion*, Cœlus whispers to the sun-god:

> O brightest of my children dear, earth-born
> And sky-engendered, Son of Mysteries
> All unrevealed even to the powers
> Which met at thy creating; at whose joys
> And palpitations sweet, and pleasures soft,
> I, Cœlus, wonder, how they came and whence;
> And at the fruits thereof what shapes they be,
> Distinct, and visible; symbols divine
> Manifestations of that beauteous life
> Diffus'd unseen throughout eternal space:
> Of these new form'd art thou, oh brightest child!
>
> (*Hyperion*, Book I, 309–319.)

Distinct and visible shapes are all " symbols divine " of " that
beauteous life " pervading the universe. This indeed smacks
of Plato.

[16] Sidney Colvin: *John Keats*, pp. 143, 145.

In the following passage from *Endymion* the idea is not so clear. Is Cynthia a reflection of things in the earth, or are earthly objects a reflection of her? After verses describing the potent influence the moon has always exerted over him, how when he was a child she seemed his sister, how she had ever been the presiding deity in all his work and play, the inspiration to all beauty and romance he has known, the poet declares:

> And as I grew in years, still didst thou blend
> With all my ardours: thou wast the deep glen;
> Thou wast the mountain-top — the sage's pen —
> The poet's harp — the voice of friends — the sun; [17]
> Thou wast the river — thou wast glory won;
> Thou wast my clarion's blast — thou wast my steed —
> My goblet full of wine — my topmost deed: —
> Thou wast the charm of women, lovely Moon!
> O what a wild and harmonized tune
> My spirit struck from all the beautiful!
>
> (*Endymion*. Book III, ll. 163–172.)

Cynthia, transcendent ideality, the essence of all reality, the Mystery, is here identified in the poet's mind with everything in the world, both material and immaterial — with mountain tops and music; with the sun and with poet's verses; with glorious deeds and the beauty of women. If all these things are but images and reflections of the ideal, then this, too, is distinctly Platonic.

The whole conception of *Endymion* must also suggest, if not Plato himself, at least the poetic Platonism of the sixteenth and seventeenth centuries. Cynthia or the moon, the supreme ideality, may be easily connected with the " heavenly beautie " and the " heavenly love " of Spenser, Herbert, Crashaw, and others — only Keats, of course, is working without reference to the religious element. Just as Keats in *Endymion* shows

---

[17] " All visible things are emblems; what thou seest is not there on its own account; strictly taken is not there at all. Matter exists only spiritually, and to represent some idea, and body it forth."
— *Sartor Resartus*. Book I, Chapter XI.

the poet in quest of highest truth, so Spenser in his hymns
prays for the Almighty

> To shed into my breast some sparkling light
> Of thine eternall Truth, that I may show
> Some little beames to mortall eyes below
> Of that immortall beautie, there with thee.
>
> *(A Hymne to Heavenly Beautie.)*

In describing the felicities that must attend ascent to the
ideal, Keats likewise portrays love as at the very " tip-top "
of the " richer entanglements " that, far more " self-destroying " than other " enthralments," lead by degrees "to the
chief intensity." Hanging by an " unseen film " as " an orbed
drop of light," it at first dazzles and confuses, but in the end,

> Melting into its radiance, we blend
> Mingle and so become a part of it.
>
> *(Endymion.* I, ll. 810–811.)

Now this would seem to be the very height of possible ethereal flight; but on the contrary, the enthralments of earthly
love are only a step toward the supremest bliss, that of union
with immortal love, for

> . . . if this earthly love has power to make
> Men's being mortal, immortal; to shake
> Ambition from their memories, and brim
> Their measure of content: what merest whim
> Seems all this poor endeavor after fame,
> To one, who keeps within his steadfast aim
> A love immortal, an immortal too.
>
> *(Endymion.* Book I, ll. 843–849.)

This immortal love then is supreme. But in spite of the fact
that human love is supposed to be a mere gradation to the
higher stage, the young poet has really left nothing more to
be said of union with heavenly essence, and we must therefore
simply take the melting, mingling, and blending in the lower
order as indicative of what occurs when the very chiefest intensity is reached. Understanding this " immortal love " as

"heavenly love" or "heavenly beauty" we need read no further than Spenser's four hymns to find a prototype in earlier
English Platonism. In Spenser, too, there is a lifting of the
soul through "love."

> From this base world unto thy heaven's light
> Where I may see those admirable things
> Which there thou workest by thy sovereign might.
>> (*Of Heavenly Love.*)

And with him, also,

> . . . Love is a celestiall harmonie
> Of likely harts composed of starres concent
> Which joyne together in sweete sympathie
> To worke ech others joy and true content.
>> (*In Honour of Beautie.*)

Moreover, to pass back for a moment to earthly love, it is
quite possible, it seems to me, to throw light on the meaning
of Keats's exclamation to Fanny Brawne in the middle days
of their courtship, " I cannot conceive any beginning of such
love as I have for you but Beauty," by referring for a moment
to certain Plato-tinctured passages from earlier English poetry.
Take, for example, this one from Drummond,

> My mind me told that in some other place
> It elsewhere saw the idea of that face,
> And lov'd a love of heavenly pure delight,
>> (*Poems. The First Part,* Sonnet VII.)

or the following from Vaughan's *A Song to Amoret,*

> For I not for an hour did love,
>> Or for a day desire,
> But with my soul had from above
>> This endless, holy fire.

These lines read in connection with Keats's sentence, inevi-
tably suggest parallel thought.

All this would seem to point rather unmistakably to the
fact that in one way or another Plato exercised a considerable
influence on the young poet.

However, striking as is the evidence, I do not find Keats's thinking consistently Platonic. He undoubtedly knew of Plato's ideal world and his " Idea," and through various channels absorbed elements of Platonism into his thought; but it would seem that, while perhaps he knew nothing of Hegelian doctrines, he is in reality much closer to Hegel than to Plato in his prevailing metaphysical conceptions.

That Keats thought of the universe as a unity, there can be no doubt; and it is quite as clear that he was confident of an existence beyond this sensuous world. Very early he has talked about the " imagination and its empyreal reflections," suggesting an unseen world to whose secrets the imagination is the only key. What the imagination seizes as truth belongs to this supersensuous reality. In the *Endymion*, we find not only that this mysterious ideality exists, but that in essence it is one with nature and with man. And the *Hyperion* suggests unity, a divine plan, and a working toward

> . . . a one far-off divine event
> To which the whole creation moves.
>
> (*In Memoriam. Last lines.*)

There is no more illuminating thought on this matter in all of Keats than that contained in the " Vale of Soul-Making " [18] letter. Here is a universe with a God who has planned so wisely that the world of circumstances he has created is exactly adapted to the making of individual identities out of the soul sparks he throws out. The highest end is the building of human souls, with fundamental, human qualities, alike in that their genesis is in God, yet distinct from each other, developed into separate individualities, and, may we say at a venture, having something of their own to contribute to the all-soul when they leave this earth and return to the enveloping bosom of the infinite. And all these creations are subject to the great moral law of the universe, an unchanging order which no voice can alter. Thus, restless Hyperion, chafing

[18] See Chapter V, *The Mystery*.

fearfully and wrathfully in the presence of his impending
doom, would fain start the day a few hours earlier —

> Fain would he have commanded, fain took throne
> And bid the day begin, if but for change.
> He might not: — No, though a primeval God:
> The sacred seasons might not be disturbed.
>   (*Hyperion*. Book I, ll. 290–293.)

Here it seems things have all been ordered from the beginning;
yet this has nothing to do with man after all, only nature, for
in Keats, we find no evidence of the doctrine of necessitarian-
ism as applied to men which early occupied the minds of
Coleridge and Wordsworth. In the idea of the " vale of Soul-
making," in spite of the part the external world plays in developing souls, it is the individual heart that, reacting on these
external impressions, always determines the direction of the
soul's growth. But unity, plan, and a spiritual super-world,
we find, were all a part of his conception.

Perhaps one of the best intimations of Keats's view can be
obtained from his letter of October, 1818, to George and
Georgiana Keats in which he discusses the abstract idea of
beauty. The poet is evidently replying to a recommendation
that he should marry:

Notwithstanding your Happiness and your recommendation, I hope
I shall never marry. Though the most beautiful Creature were waiting for me at the end of a Journey or a Walk; though the Carpets
were of Silk, the Curtains of the morning Clouds; the chairs and
Sofa stuffed with Cygnet's down; the food Manna, the Wine beyond
Claret, the window opening on Winander mere I should not feel — or
rather my Happiness would not be so fine, as my Solicitude is sublime. Then instead of what I have described there is a sublimity to
welcome me home. The roaring of the wind is my wife, and the
Stars through the window pane are my Children. The mighty abstract Idea I have of Beauty in all things stifles the more divided and
minute domestic happiness — an amiable wife and sweet Children I
contemplate as a part of that Beauty, but I must have a thousand
of these beautiful particles to fill up my heart. I feel more and
more every day, as my imagination strengthens, that I do not live in

this world alone but in a thousand ,orlds. No sooner am I alone than shapes of epic greatness are stationed around me, and serve my Spirit the office which is equivalent to a King's bodyguard — then, "Tragedy with sceptered pall comes sweeping by." According to my state of mind I am with Achilles shouting in the Trenches, or with Theocritus in the Vales of Sicily. Or I throw my whole being into Troilus, and repeating those lines, 'I wander like a lost Soul upon the Stygian Banks staying for waftage,' I melt into the air with a voluptuousness so delicate that I am content to be alone.

The "mighty abstract Idea of Beauty" here appears to be an imaginative conception of a concrete reality of which the things of this world are an integral part, yet only a small portion of the whole. Keats can contemplate a wife and children as a part of that Beauty, but only as particles of which it takes a thousand to fill his heart. It is to be noted, however, that the things of the purely imaginative reality take their color from the known actuality of the world; not as reflections nor as prototypes, but as elements akin in nature, and all by the same spirit interfused, behind all the sense of the sublime and the mysterious. There is little of Plato in this abstract idea of beauty; there is in it a nearer approach to the Hegelian theory of the Absolute. Keats is too conscious of the world in which he lives — the actual, the present — as a vital part of the ideal to be consistently Platonic. We have seen how his thinking drove him more and more to turn to the actual as the basic principle in his scheme of poetic salvation. To be sure, the sensuously real is merely a starting point upon which he constructs his imaginative universe, but there must be always that point of departure, and, too, it is in itself ever a part, however small, of the absolute unity that is reached, not merely a symbol of it.

This instinctive insistence on beginning with and building on the actual possibly saved Keats from wandering afield into an abstract mysticism or into a philosophic haze of exaggerated ideality, with "no earthly depth to root in." It was leading him to a poetry whose central theme would be humanity, with a warp and woof of the character, sentiment, and passions of mankind, yet with the divine touch of eternal truth upon it, within it the breath and spirit of the infinite.

To Keats, the secret of the ability to penetrate into the very borderlands of being, which is the poet's field, is to know life and the world about us to the depths, and especially to have entered into its pain. And knowing this, we have the light which illuminates all the dark and hidden passages that lead to the " Penetralium of mystery," to the heart of the whole universe; by knowing this world, we know the inner spirit of all; for all are of one substance joined. And this gives us our right clue to Keats's conception of the relation between this world of sense and the invisible real in the realm of poetry and art.

To Shelley the actual things of the world were a veil to the hidden reality and harmony of the universe, to Plato they were a sign and a symbol, to Hegel they were an extension, but to Keats they were both an extension and a revelation. Keats was a philosophical idealist to whom divine and eternal laws become apparent through visible and present phenomena, themselves both a part and a manifestation of absolute reality and truth. He was as distinctly this when in *Endymion* he made the sensuous, the deeply human, and ideality one, as when he gave *The Fall of Hyperion* to the world. It was a settled tenet of his metaphysical faith.

From the foregoing, it will be seen that Keats's conception of beauty was on a higher plane than has often been supposed. To him beauty is the subjective reaction to a glimpse beyond the veil. It is truth — truth made to live through the power of a creative imagination able to dissolve the flying vapors of intangible substance into reality, or truth seized through the power of the re-creative imagination capable of reconstructing the images with which an original artist has wrought. The rulership of the universe is to fall to that power most strong in beauty, that is, most strong in the god-like capacity to seize and apprehend truth through the intellectualized, educated intuitive faculties; even so did the Apollo-Neptune dynasty triumph over the Titans. Finally, this beauty is eternal: it is of the everlasting reality that lies behind the mere surface and seeming of earthly things; whoever has imaginative power sufficient to grasp it, has laid hold of permanent, indestructible truth; he has enjoyed, moreover, the highest type of aesthetic experience — he has known Beauty face to face.

CHAPTER IX

PRINCIPLES AND PRACTICE

I

" In poetry I have sought to avoid system and mannerism,"
wrote Shelley to Keats. " I wish those who excel me in genius
would pursue the same plan." Shelley's indirect advice is
aimed at Keats, as a part of the little interchange of mutual
admonition that went on between the two poets. Shelley had
advised Keats not to publish his " first blights on Hampstead Heath," and had later invited him to visit him at Marlow. But the young poet did not accept the advice nor the
invitation. He gave as his reason for refusing to visit Shelley
during the composition of *Endymion* his desire to " have his
own unfettered scope." And now, as if a little nettled at
Shelley's implication, he includes in his reply, along with
some humble acknowledgment of debt for former counsel it is
true, a bit of gratuitous advice to the elder poet. The " poor
poem " mentioned in Keats's opening sentence is *Endymion,*
which Shelley had recently re-read, " with a new sense of the
treasure of poetry it contains."

I am glad you take any pleasure in my poor poem, which I would
willingly take the trouble to unwrite, if possible, did I care so much
as I have done about reputation. I received a copy of the *Cenci,* as
from yourself, from Hunt. There is only one part of it I am judge
of — the poetry and dramatic effect, which by many spirits now-a-
days is considered the Mammon. A modern work, it is said, must
have a purpose, which may be the God. An artist must serve
Mammon; he must have " self-concentration " — selfishness, perhaps.
You, I am sure, will forgive me for sincerely remarking that you
might curb your magnanimity, and be more of an artist, and load
every rift of your subject with ore. The thought of such discipline
must fall like cold chains upon you, who perhaps never sat with your

wings furled for six months together. And is not this extraordinary talk for the writer of *Endymion,* whose mind was like a pack of scattered cards? I am picked up and sorted to a pip. My imagination is a monastery, and I am its monk. . . . I remember you advising me not to express my first blights, on Hampstead Heath. I am returning advice upon your hands. Most of the poems in the volume [1] I send you have been written above two years, and would never have been published but for the hope of gain; so you see I am inclined enough to take your advice now.

This letter is interesting and valuable, not only for the direct artistic principle expressed in the injunction to the poet to load every rift of his subject with ore, but for the confession to a capitulation to something like Shelley's way of thinking as to the badness of the first poems and to a coincident development in Keats's own ideas in regard to technical merit in a work of art. The sentence, " The thought of such discipline must fall like cold chains upon you, who perhaps never sat with your wings furled for six months together," recalls Keats's metaphoric description of his periods of moulting.[2] In such periods of intense reflection and self-examination he had repudiated many of those " mannerisms " and much of the " system " that Shelley deplores. The Hunt-Beattie-Mrs. Tighe influences had early been discredited, and some of his early verse mannerisms partly borrowed from Hunt he had discarded even before *Endymion* was written. The reason was probably a developed taste to which his own rigorous reasoning and a continued study of his poetic masters contributed much. " No one," writes Cowden Clarke, than whom no one knew more of Keats's real self, " could chastise his thoughts more earnestly than Keats." And Professor Saintsbury, in his discussion of Keats in *The History of English Prosody,* attributes his growth in poetic taste to the study of Milton and Shakespeare — " who, as has been said, are between them sufficient to destroy all prosodic error." At any rate, long before his death, Keats had learned to apply to himself the wise suggestion of Longinus contained in his

[1] The *Lamia-Hyperion* Volume.　　　　[2] See Chapter I, p. 27.

epigrammatic dictum, " Genius may sometimes want the spur, but it stands as frequently in need of the curb," and had sincerely undertaken to impose upon himself the severest self-restraint.

Unlike many of the romantic school of thinkers, Schiller for example, Keats did not put form above substance, but the reverse. To him matter was chief, though he quite realized that only in a perfect marriage of form and content could beauty be expressed. Keats understood thoroughly the necessity of mastering the technique of his art. When he urged Shelley to be more of an artist, and load every rift of his subject with ore, he was thinking partly of the art side of poetry. To Keats much of Shelley's verse must have appeared diffuse, vague, and meaningless. Shelley needed discipline in thought and expression, the same discipline to which Keats himself was ever subjecting his muse.

What Keats earnestly sought for was exact veracity in expressing his conception of reality. His aim, as A. Clutton-Brock, writing in the *John Keats Memorial Volume,* says, was to express this reality, " to draw everything in its peculiarity, which, he believed, was its beauty. That was why he looked upon ' fine phrases like a lover,' not merely and vaguely for their sound, but because a fine phrase meant for him a sharp drawing, the rhythmical drawing of poetry in which the very momentum defines and expresses."

Keats's ears were attuned with exquisite sensibility to beauty of language and rhythm, but with regard to sound and sense, in spite of all that has been said to the contrary, he loved sound chiefly for its power to project sense on its right way. " A melodious passage in poetry," he says, " is full of pleasures both sensual and spiritual. The spiritual is felt when the very letters and points of charactered language show like the hieroglyphics of beauty ; the mysterious signs of our immortal freemasonry ! ' A thing to dream of, not to tell.' " Even when he speaks of what he calls the " sensual " quality, he seems to be thinking of the expression of the inner emotional, rather than of purely sensuous, effects: "The sensual life of verse springs warm from the lips of Kean and to one learned in Shakespearian hieroglyphics — learned in the spiritual portion of those lines to which Kean adds a sensual grandeur; his tongue must seem to have robbed the Hybla bees and left them honeyless! There is an indescribable *gusto* in his voice, by which we feel that the utterer is speaking of the past and future while speaking of the instant. When he says in Othello, 'Put up your bright swords, for the dew will rust them,' we feel that his throat had commanded where swords were as thick as reeds. From eternal risk, he speaks as though his body were unassailable. Again, his exclamation of 'blood, blood, blood!' is direful and slaughterous to the deepest degree; the very words appear stained and gory." All this is indeed but further testimony to the poet's instinctive demand for the word and phrase of deep suggestive power, for expression that rings true to the heart's deepest emotions, and to his native response to the beauty of true organic rhythm.

Keats did indeed love "fine phrases." "There is a cool pleasure in the very sound of vale," he exclaimed rapturously, in writing of Milton's *Paradise Lost*. "Milton has put vales in heaven and hell with the very utter affection and yearning of a great Poet." And in a letter to Woodhouse, September, 1819, he includes a few lines from *Hyperion* "on account of a word in the last line of a fine sound." The line is,

> Though it blows legend-laden through the trees,

and the word, as one would guess, is "legend-laden." In a letter to Fanny Brawne, July, 1819, there is a sentence that throws light on Keats's sensitive feeling for language. He is trying to express his love and admiration. "I want a brighter word than bright, a fairer word than fair," he exclaims. As Mr. Draper says in comment, in his article in the Memorial Volume, "'*Bright*' and '*fair*' are words that have been used a long time in the world, and have been taken for granted:

they are signs, but are not any longer expressions of what men have felt." The poet-lover wants a word newly-minted that will exactly and completely carry the sense of the vivid emotion that wells within him.

It was this exquisite feeling for freshly lucent language that enabled Keats to write with the marvelous felicity of phrase that marks the works of his maturity. How his mind worked in its search for the right expression we may see from the emendations he made in reworking his poems. In Mr. de Selincourt's admirable editions and in Mr. Forman's *Prose and Poetry of John Keats*, containing variations in reading in manuscripts, one may study his revisions in detail. There is not space to go far into these here. But to note only two or three examples from the matchless *Ode to a Nightingale* is sufficient to show the delicacy and accuracy of taste which guided the poet in his search for perfection in organic rhythm. In the opening line, " a drowsy numbness pains " first read " a painful numbness falls "; in the second stanza " Cool'd a long age " was first " Cooling an age "; and the almost indescribably exquisite " Forlorn " in the eighth stanza was added in the second draft, a repetitive effect of inimitable melancholic beauty. The change in each case is toward a fine rightness, a closer harmony of sound and sense. A hint as to the principles that guided the young poet in his selection of words and sounds in verse building is to be had from Benjamin Bailey's memoranda:

One of his favorite topics of discourse was the principle of melody in verse, upon which he had his own notions, particularly in the management of open and close vowels. I think I have seen a somewhat similar theory attributed to Mr. Wordsworth. . . . It was, that the vowels should be so managed as not to clash one with another, so as to hear the melody, — and yet that they should be interchanged, like differing notes of music to prevent monotony.[3]

Keats's delight in the music of beautiful verse, where sound and sense unite in forms of loveliness, finds constant expres-

[3] Memoranda of Benjamin Bailey, Houghton MSS. Quoted by Colvin, in *John Keats*, p. 147.

sion in his remarks on other poets. On the blank space at the end of the " Floure and The Lefe " he wrote:

> Oh! what a power has white simplicity!
> What mighty power has this gentle story!

And in the Marginalia to his *Paradise Lost*, apropos of the rhythm of the verse, was penned this comment:

> Heaven moves on like music throughout. Hell is also peopled with angels; it also moves on like music, not grating and harsh, but like a grand accompaniment in the Base to Heaven.

In sound and phrase and sense, merged and dissolved into one single harmony, each fitted to each as if by nature formed, as in the best of Milton, Keats found supreme aesthetic satisfaction.

In his own verse, he strove for this effect. Knowing that poetic beauty is dependent on an emotional arousal, a mental excitation attuned to the key of imaginative perception, his great care was for rhythmic forms so adequately adapted to a vital and beautiful expression of the mood and thought as to satisfy the demands of his exacting inner ear, and, moreover, to reproduce in the mind of the reader the exact images he sought to convey. What Keats wanted was to make the reader live the scene imaginatively, to feel it. And to achieve this end he sought ever to make his verse express what he called " the voice of true feeling."

II

In the *John Keats Memorial Volume* of 1921, there is a contribution in verse by Amy Lowell that seems to be expressive of her idea of Keats's attitude toward the art of poetry. It begins:

> Well, John Keats,
> I know how you felt when you swung out of the inn
> And started up Box Hill after the moon.

Then it continues with the ecstatic emotions which the poet felt in contact with the moon, how he gloried in her loveliness, until she finally slipped through his hand and left him " tortured with this anguish of unbearable beauty." After that Keats went home and wrote and wrote by a wavering candle, and finally as he " tumbled into bed " he said: " It's a piece of luck I thought of coming out to Box Hill."

As if Keats were the most veritable hac*r* writer scouting for a thrill and a punch for his sensational feature next day! But the less Keats he, and the less Amy Lowell she, if either one ever depended upon such " luck " for the inspiration to poetry. No, Keats was not out like a Sunday supplement writer looking for tips and thrills.

It was in silent, deep communion that his spirit wrought upon the materials of the world and transmuted them into poetic beauty. The account of Charles Brown as to the source and evolution of the " *Ode to a Nightingale* " is authentic evidence on this point:

> In the spring of 1819 a nightingale had built her nest near my house. Keats felt a tranquil and continued joy in her song; and one morning he took his chair from the breakfast table to the grass plot under a plum tree, where he sat for two or three hours. When he came into the house, I perceived he had some scraps of paper in his hand, and these he was quietly thrusting behind the books. On inquiry, I found those scraps, four or five in number, contained his poetic feeling on the song of our nightingale.

It was thus that with quiet, observant soul Keats waited upon life for truth and his own sincere reactions to it.

Superficiality and insincerity of any kind the young poet hated with all his soul. Such a character as Byron's, for example, seems to have irritated him; Byron's egoism, his eternal pose, his coxcombry, all in direct contrast to Keats's own simple honesty, were at times extremely distasteful to him. An interesting expression of this is to be found in an incident recorded by Severn. When Keats and Severn were on their way to Italy during Keats's illness, they were overtaken by a violent storm. " After the tempest had subsided, Keats was reading the description of the storm in Don Juan, and cast the book on the floor in a transport of indignation. ' How horrible an example of human nature,' he cried, ' is this man, who has no pleasure left him but to gloat over and jeer at the most awful incidents .of life. Oh! this is a paltry originality, which consists in making solemn things gay, and gay things solemn, and yet it will fascinate thousands, by the very diabolical outrage of their sympathies. Byron's perverted education makes him assume to feel, and try to impart to others those depraved sensations which the want of any education excites in many.' " [4]

Keats craved truth. And since to him the most truth is to be discovered through the emotions and intuitions, his career was one earnest quest for authentic poetic feeling. He was impatient with superficiality; he delighted in the genuine. This attitude is voiced in Endymion's distressed cry,[5] " I have no depth to strike in "; it is apparent in Keats's dissatisfaction with himself for his lack of first-hand experience and his determination to seek knowledge expressed in the early 1818 letters; and there is abundant other evidence of it in his writings. Of his own work he once declared, " My poetry will never be fit for anything; it doesn't cover its ground well." Of Wordsworth he wrote severely, in commenting on his Gypsy, " It seems to me that if Wordsworth had thought a little deeper at that moment, he would not have written the poem at all." In other words he is accusing Wordsworth of superficiality. " I should judge it," he continues, " to have been written in one of the most comfortable moods of his life — it is a kind of sketchy intellectual landscape, not a search after truth." Keats required of himself this search for truth, and was on his guard against the entrance into his writing of any element that seemed hostile to it — for instance, foreign

[4] Houghton: Life and Letters of John Keats. Universal Library Edition, p. 259.
[5] Book II, l. 161.

idioms. Native words, he felt, are most expressive of English life and thought. Upon this subject he writes emphatically:

I shall never become attached to a foreign idiom, so as to put it into my writings. The Paradise Lost, though so fine in itself, is a corruption of our language. It should be kept as it is, unique, a curiosity, a beautiful and grand curiosity, the most remarkable production of the world; a northern dialect accommodating itself to Greek and Latin inversions and intonations. The purest English, I think — or what ought to be the purest — is Chatterton's. The language had existed long enough to be entirely incorrupted of Chaucer's Gallicisms, and still the old words are used. Chatterton's language is entirely Northern. I prefer the native music of it to Milton's, cut by feet. . . . Miltonic verse cannot be written, but is the verse of art. I wish to devote myself to another verse alone.

" Miltonic verse cannot be written but is the verse of art." Whatever Keats means by " cannot be written," it is clear enough that when he says " Miltonic verse . . . is the verse of art," he is declaring that it will not do for him; he is instinctively setting against " a verse of art," a verse best fitted to express deep, true feeling. That becomes clear from a second more explicit utterance on the same subject:

No I will not copy a parcel of verses. I always somehow associate Chatterton with autumn. He is the purest writer in the English Language. He has no French idiom or particles, like Chaucer — 'tis genuine English Idiom in English words. I have given up Hyperion — there were too many Miltonic inversions in it. Miltonic verse cannot be written but in an artful, or, rather artist's humour. I wish to give myself up to other sensations. English ought to be kept up. It may be interesting to you to pick out some lines from Hyperion, and put a mark + to the false beauty proceeding from art and one || to the true voice of feeling. Upon my soul 'twas imagination — I cannot make the distinction. Every now and then there is a Miltonic intonation. But I cannot make the division properly.

Professor Cook declares in his *Art of Poetry,* " The imitable and compassable qualities of a work of art are always matters of detail, rarely or never the vital and animating principle. Hence where grandeur is present in a composition, it springs directly from the soul of the artist. Taking thought will add no cubit to the moral stature of the thinker, and just as little to that of his literary product." In *Hyperion*, Keats had taken thought as to his literary product by deliberately studying Milton and seeking heights of sublimity by modelling his verse to some extent after the form of the older poet. But this touch of borrowed grandeur irked Keats; his sensitive feeling for faithful and truthful expression of his own deepest self was offended.

Keats had discovered that, for him at least, the Miltonic manner was productive of artificiality; to write in this fashion simply meant " art for art's sake " rather than art for the sake of expressing simply and sincerely the thought and emotions of the heart. His suggestion, " and put a mark + to the false beauty proceeding from art, and one || to the true voice of feeling," tells the whole story. In itself it is worth a volume of critical comment on the high-minded seriousness with which Keats viewed his art.

In the quotations just cited, there is contained, it seems to me, the most logical explanation to be found for Keats's giving up the first *Hyperion*. Many foolish conjectures have been made by various critics, but here is the secret. Keats felt that in following false fires he was prostituting his art, and had no heart to go on. In his essay entitled *The Second Version of Hyperion* in the Memorial Volume, Lascelles Abercrombie has put the matter nicely and precisely. There was nothing wrong with the subject in the first *Hyperion*, he explains; the real trouble was, " The splendours had become *decoration.* . . . And in the instant he realized that he was not getting complete and precise expression for his inspiration, he discarded the poem, and started again. There is no clearer or more poignant instance of the artistic conscience than this. It was the grandest piece of blank verse since *Samson Agonistes* that Keats thus so sternly discarded." And that was it. Keats felt that he was sacrificing truth and clarity in the interests of false art, that is, false for him, for it was not his native mode of expression. Therefore, he determined to abandon his first version and start anew. It is illuminating, in the light of this fact, to note that Keats evidently began the *Revision of Hyperion* with the intention of saying what he had to say clearly enough and adequately enough so that people could not fail to understand. He could not do that in the Miltonic verse of art, so he determined upon a radical revision.

It is worth noting here in parenthesis that in giving up the Miltonic style, Keats is not giving up Milton. Always, Milton stands next to Shakespeare in the affections of the youthful poet. Keats simply came to realize that the ultimate verse form he was seeking in his struggle for perfect harmony of content and expression did not lie in the Miltonic direction. For him Miltonic verse could not be organic, hence his use of it approached the merely rhetorical.

Even in the sometimes extravagantly phrased, often mawkish *Endymion,* Keats had consciously worked for naturalness and truth in speech. If he failed it was due to defect in reach, not to lack of true vision of the thing to be attained. His own comment sets forth his ideal:

Leigh Hunt I showed my 1st Book to — He allows it not much merit as a whole; says it is unnatural and made ten objections to it in the mere skimming over. He says the conversation is unnatural and too high-flown for Brother and Sister, — says it should be simple, forgetting do ye mind that they are both overshadowed by a supernatural Power, and of force could not speak like Francesca in the "Rimini." He must first prove that Caliban's poetry is unnatural. This with me completely overturns his objections.

All good proof that what Keats sought was the true voice of feeling.

One of the most striking comments on Keats's artistic conscience and its scrupulous regard for depth and sincerity as opposed to the mawkish is to be found in the interesting letter to Woodhouse recently unearthed by Miss Amy Lowell and contributed to the *John Keats Memorial Volume* in 1921.

Woodhouse has been urging Keats to publish. The poet replies,

> I will give you a few reasons why I shall persist in not publishing The Pot of Basil. It is too smokeable. I can get it smoak'd at the Carpenters shaving chimney much more cheaply. There is too much inexperience of line, and simplicity of Knowledge in it — which might do very well after one's death, but not while one is alive. There are very few would look to the reality. I intend to use more finesse with the Public. It is possible to write fine things which cannot be laugh'd at in any way. Isabella is what I should call were I a reviewer "A weak-sided Poem" with an amusing sober-sadness about it. Not that I do not think Reynolds and you are quite right about it — it is enough for me. But this will not do to be public. If I may say so, in my dramatic capacity I enter fully into the feeling: but in Propria Persona I should be apt to quiz it myself. There is no objection of this kind to Lamia — A good deal to St. Agnes Eve — only not so glaring. Would as I say I could write you something sylvestian. But I have no time to think: I am an otiosus-preoccupatus Man. I think upon crutches like the folks in your Pump room.

The trouble with *Isabella*, Keats is saying, was its thinness: there was too little poetic power displayed in its making; there was "too much inexperience of line and simplicity of knowledge in it." He had not really in his proper self entered into the feeling of it all; hence the weak-sidedness of the poem. Writing to Taylor, September 20, 1819, Woodhouse speaks of Keats's attitude toward *Isabella:* "He said he could not bear the former (*Isabella*) now. It appeared to him mawkish." *The Eve of St. Agnes* too suffered somewhat from this same defect — too many of its phrases were mere drapery and decoration. But *Lamia* was better.[6] It was "the voice of true feeling." That was probably why Keats was so sure it would give people a "sensation," and sensation, he declared, is what they want in poetry.

6 Mr. Fausset says, "A letter recently published by Miss Amy Lowell shows with what a ruthless sense of values he dismissed *Lamia* and *The Eve of St. Agnes* to the haunts of prettiness and sentimentality." (P. 65.) But Keats does not so condemn *Lamia* and the *Eve of St. Agnes.* Indeed, the statement, "There is no objection of this kind to *Lamia*," shows that Keats places the poem entirely above the region of "prettiness and sentimentality."

I have been reading over a part of a short poem I have composed lately, called Lamia, and I am certain there is that sort of fire in it which must take hold of people in some way. Give them either pleasant or unpleasant sensation — what they want is a sensation of some sort.

"What they want is a sensation." And in the sense he meant it, yes. Enthusiasm, "transport," Longinus would have called this quality — the one valid test for literature. Keats knew that warm response can be had from the readers only when the poet himself has felt deeply and seen truly, and is capable of clothing his vision in language of simplicity and power. It takes fire to draw fire; it requires "the true voice of feeling" to arouse the glow of warm emotional response.

III

Spontaneity, ease, and fitness of expression became with Keats an eager passion which led him to discontent with the old and outworn and drove him on ever in restless quest for faultless forms in which to clothe his thought.

It was in this spirit that he tried for an improved sonnet arrangement. "I have been endeavoring to discover a better Sonnet Stanza than we have," he explains in a letter to George and Georgiana Keats. "The legitimate does not suit the language over well from the pouncing rhymes — the other appears too elegiac — and the couplet at the end of it has seldom a pleasing effect — I do not pretend to have succeeded — it will explain itself." And another time, he encloses the verses entitled *Ever let the Fancy roam* and *Bards of passion and of mirth*, with the comment:

These are specimens of a sort of rondeau which I think I shall become partial to — because you have one idea amplified with greater ease and more delight and freedom than in the sonnet.

Thus Keats went on through all his working days studying the old forms, selecting, rejecting, ever seeking to adapt and fashion his expression to meet the requirements of fresh vision and fine taste. From *I Stood Tip-Toe* to *Endymion;* from *Endymion* to the Odes; from the Odes to the final revision of *Hyperion,* the search continued. Sometimes feverishly, but patiently and painstakingly, the young poet labored at his great task. The important truth that art must be experimental, that mastery cannot come at a single bound, but that, as Björkman says, " Art must wrestle with its technique, conquer its material before it can center on its final and true mission," was one of the principles that Keats adopted in his theory of poetry. He eagerly sought perfection, but his good judgment told him that a final marriage of perfect form to substance can come only after much struggle, only after many trials and failures have schooled the creative and critical faculties to a higher reach and a firmer grasp. The necessity for experimentation is delightfully expressed in what I like to call the Snailhorn Perception of Beauty letter. Keats is writing to Haydon in April, 1818.

Believe me Haydon your picture is part of myself — I have ever been too sensible of the labyrinthian path to eminence in Art (judging from Poetry) ever to think I understood the emphasis of painting. The innumerable compositions and decompositions which take place between the intellect and its thousand materials before it arrives at that trembling delicate and snail-horn perception of beauty. I know not your many havens of intenseness — nor ever can know them: but for this I hope nought you achieve is lost upon me; for when a Schoolboy the abstract Idea I had of an heroic painting — was what I cannot describe. I saw it sometimes sideways, large, prominent, round and colour'd with magnificence — somewhat like the feel I have of Anthony and Cleopatra. Or of Alcibiades leaning on his Crimson Couch in his Galley, his broad shoulders imperceptibly heaving with the Sea.

May we not believe that in this passage we have a pretty clear exposition of Keats's idea of the creation of any art form from the artist's standpoint? Given an intellect with its " thousand materials " to work with, — with images on one hand, and, on the other, sensuous symbols: in poetry, words and metrical relations; in painting, lines and color; in music, sounds in rhythmical arrangements, — there is a necessity for a long struggle for a fitting form, which, when attained, is not only a perfect expression of the imaginative beauty sought, but is, moreover, a means of the artist's coming to a true intuition of that beauty, "that trembling, delicate and snail-horn perception," Keats describes. Only with true expression can come true perception. This is the completed fabric of the creative imagination — the moment of realization of the identity of form with content, of beauty with truth.

How are we to reconcile this idea with what Keats has written elsewhere, " That if poetry comes not as naturally as the leaves to a tree, it had better not come at all " ?   There may be some explanation in the fact that this second idea was expressed two months earlier than the first. Keats was growing rapidly in these days — in the spring of 1818 — and these two passages might indicate a changed attitude. But I believe we need find no such great discrepancy as to make this belief necessary. Possibly these compositions and decompositions he mentions may occur in the mind of the artist before they are set down in any symbols whatever. *Endymion,* for instance, which, Benjamin Bailey tells us, was written steadily and rapidly, so much a day, with as much ease as one could write prose, probably grew out of long periods of reflection in some of those days when Keats " thought so much about poetry, so long together," that he " could not get to sleep at night." At such times, no doubt, the formative process went on in much the same manner as he has described it to Haydon.

Moreover, we know that to some extent there was, as he wrote *Endymion,* a gradual unfolding of the Beauty, the imaginative idea, for which he was striving. We have seen how in writing to his publisher, John Taylor, concerning the lines on happiness in Book I, he had declared that this whole passage was, when he wrote it, " a regular stepping of the Imagination towards a truth," that his having written this argument would perhaps be the greatest service to him of anything he had ever done, for, he says, "It set before me the gradations of happiness, even like a kind of pleasure thermometer, and is my first step towards the chief attempt in the drama. The playing of different natures with joy and sorrow."

Again, of *Endymion* as a whole, while itself written off rapidly without apparent testing and revision in a search for true expression, Keats realized it was but one of the attempts among the numerous " compositions and decompositions " necessary to an approach toward his ideal. " It is just that this youngster should die away," he wrote in his preface to *Endymion:* " a sad thought for me, if I had not some hope that while it is dwindling I may be plotting, and fitting myself for verses fit to live."

To be intelligently self-critical, to be ever on the alert to detect elements of weakness and strength, only so may a poet truly realize his largest self. Keats, unlike Wordsworth, was fortunate enough to be endowed with sound critical sense. Hence the great value of his experiments. On the subject of criticism he declares manfully:

I cannot but feel indebted to those gentlemen who have taken my part. As for the rest, I begin to get a little acquainted with my own strength and weakness. — Praise or blame has but a momentary effect on the man whose love of beauty in the abstract makes him a severe critic on his own Works. My own domestic criticism has given me pain without comparison beyond what Blackwood or the Quarterly could possibly inflict — and also when I feel that I am right, no external praise can give me such a glow as my own solitary reperception and ratification of what is fine. . . . The Genius of Poetry must work out its own salvation in a man: It cannot be matured by law and precept, but by sensation and watchfulness in itself. That which is creative must create itself.

These ideas of the necessity for experiments in art and the function of such trials in his development as a poet appear clearly in various enlightening remarks on *Endymion*. Writing to Benjamin Bailey in October, 1817, Keats says:

As to what you say about my being a Poet, I can return no Answer but by saying that the high Idea I have of poetical fame makes me think I see it towering too high above me. At any rate, I have no right to talk until Endymion is finished, it will be a test, a trial of my Powers of Imagination, and chiefly of my invention which is a rare thing indeed — by which I must make 4000 lines of one bare circumstance, and fill them with poetry — and when I consider that this is a great task, and that when done it will take me but a dozen paces towards the temple of fame — it makes me say — God forbid that I should be without such a task!

Quite as illuminating are these additional extracts from the letter to James Augustus Hessey, already partially quoted:

In " Endymion," I leaped headlong into the sea, and thereby have become better acquainted with the Soundings, the quicksands, and the rocks, than if I had stayed upon the green shore and piped a silly pipe. . . . Had I been nervous about its being a perfect piece, and with that view asked advice and trembled over every page, it would not have been written.

Endymion was to be a test, a trial of his powers, yet it was but a preparation for greater things to come. " If Endymion serves me as a pioneer," he wrote to John Taylor, " perhaps I ought to be content." And again, with level sanity and calm judgment, rating his first long poem at its true worth, he declared to Haydon:

My Ideas with respect to it I assure you are very low — and I would write the subject thoroughly again — but I am tired of it and think the time would be better spent in writing a new Romance which I have in my eye for next summer — Rome was not built in a Day — and all the good I expect from my employment this summer is the fruit of Experience which I hope to gather in my next Poem.

As late as March, 1819, he is writing to George and Georgiana Keats:

I am, however, young, writing at random, straining at particles of light in the midst of a great darkness, without knowing the bearing of any one assertion, of any one opinion.

Though most of *Hyperion* and some of the great odes had been written before this, Keats's search for the ideal beauty of form and content had not yet resulted satisfactorily. With humility and good sense he had striven to attain it, but when he gave over the task of revising *Hyperion* he was still far from content. What he sought was a union of free form with grandeur and sublimity of substance. *Endymion* was free, but it was not sublime. *Hyperion* was grand, but it was not free.

In the poetry Keats has left us we find two almost distinct methods: there is, on one hand, the extravagant freedom and the excess of imagery and detail of *I Stood Tip-Toe, Endymion,* and *The Eve of St. Agnes;* on the other, is the chaste severity and restraint of the *Hyperion, To Autumn,* and *The Eve of St. Mark.* The *Endymion* manner, Keats early saw, was all too unrestrained, and before he came to *Lamia,* his next long narrative poem, he had prepared himself against his earlier faults by a careful preliminary study of Dryden. In *Isabella* and *The Eve of St. Agnes,* which had come between, he had sternly held himself within bounds by fitting each into the moulds of a set form, and, though both are done in the earlier free style, he had in them achieved a distinct advance in control. As a reward for his pains in preparation, he secured in *Lamia* what must have been a near approach to that ideal he sought. For here is an easy flowing narrative movement, lyric in tone, yet held within the confines of the couplet form, free from both the formal precision of Dryden and the objectionable enjambement and unbridled excess of *Endymion.* The result is a verse of power and delight, admirably adapted to the lyric tale he here relates.

Before this had come the *Hyperion* experiment. Milton was now the model, and for the first time Keats tried the blank verse of the great masters of English poetry. Here was restraint and to spare. But the sober Miltonic latinisms did not please the fastidious Keats; they fettered and shackled his free spirit. "I have but lately stood on my guard against Milton," we find him declaring. "Life to him would be death to me." In the *Revision* he tried to amend what seemed to him the artificiality of *Hyperion* by letting out the reins a little in a manner more his own. But even here he could not please himself, and soon gave over the attempt entirely.

In the meantime, however, Keats had written the great 1819 odes, subjecting himself to the severe discipline of established form, yet allowing himself the freedom and independence necessary to achieve distinct individual effects. The odes are quietly chaste in tone, yet richly luxuriant in thought and imagery; they are sober, yet magnificent; restrained, but gloriously free. Here, I think, and in *Lamia*, Keats had most nearly found himself. Had he gone on writing, it would probably have been in a verse similar to that of these poems of the middle manner, the excrescences of *Endymion* pruned away, the austerity of *Hyperion* relaxed into forms of rich, abundant beauty. Only this we cannot know. Sad that this most gifted singer should never have been given opportunity to go beyond the experimental stage. Yet how marvellous those experiments!

IV

" The Genius of Poetry must work out its own salvation in a man." Here Keats is declaring for a doctrine of poetic independence that he amply upholds in other utterances. No matter how much suggestion he has received from contemporary poets, Keats is saying, no matter how servilely he may have followed the masters in the period of raw apprenticeship, the true poet must in the end break his own paths and work his way to his destined goal in his own individual fashion. Keats well knew that he himself might be justly charged with lack of originality in his maiden days — the stamp of Spenser, Hunt, and others was only too plainly marked upon his early verses. But by the time he began *Endymion* he had obviously resolved upon complete emancipation. As we have seen, Shelley had invited him to visit him while he was writing the poem; but, jealously intent upon guarding his precious originality, the young poet had refused.

After *Endymion* was finished, it seems he was ready to resent vigorously any charge of outside influences imputed to him in the process of creating the poem. "You see, Bailey," he wrote, "how independent my Writing has been, Hunt's dissuasion was of no avail — I refused to visit Shelley that I might have my own unfettered scope; — and after all, I shall have the Reputation of Hunt's élève. His corrections and amputations will by the knowing ones be traced in the Poem. This is, to be sure, the vexation of a day. . . ." The studious care with which Keats had avoided Hunt and Shelley during the composition of *Endymion* may be inferred from a passage from a later letter in which the young poet is smarting a bit under the sting of undoubtedly well-meant criticisms from Hunt. Keats is writing to his brothers George and Thomas. "The fact is he and Shelley are hurt, and perhaps justly, at my not having showed them the affair officiously and from several hints I have had they appear much disposed to dissect and anatomize any trip or slip I may have made." This was, quite likely, unfounded suspicion, for Shelley and Hunt seem to have had a genuine desire to befriend their young brother genius at every opportunity; but it at least corroborates other testimony to the effect that Keats worked on his first long poem with the nearest to absolute independence possible.

Later he went to Milton for a partial model, but him alsc he forswore, and, if, as certain critics believe, he still later was turning to Dante for guidance, it is pretty certain he would have deserted him too. For Keats's convictions, once formed, were strong. And one of his firmest beliefs was that the poet must permit himself "his own unfettered scope." He wanted to write independently of popular opinion, and he declared, "I feel it in my power to refuse the poisonous suffrage of a public"; he wanted to write independently of the reviewers, and he spoke bravely of the difficulties involved, "for the Reviews have enervated and made indolent men's minds," until "few think for themselves"; he wanted to write independently of tradition, and he confessed, "One of my Ambitions is to make as great a revolution in modern dramatic writing as Kean has done in acting — Another, to upset the drawling of the blue-stocking literary world." Independence seemed the one condition to his poetic salvation. And it was not a silly self-vaunting egotism that had bred this view; it was not a cheap desire for the bizarre and different — Keats was always willing to learn all the past had to teach: it came rather as a result of a deep insight into the fundamental principle that to write with truth, and sincerity, and power, a poet must always speak from the deepest wells of his most vital self. So Keats declared, " I will write independently. I have written independently *without Judgment*. I may write independently and *with Judgment* hereafter."

V

Keats many times expressed a desire to be of use to the world; his ideal was service, performed in a natural, unassuming way — to do the world some good but not to preach. " I am convinced more and more every day that (excepting the human friend philosopher), a fine writer is the most genuine being in the world." When Keats said that, he was placing the human friend philosopher above even the poet. But a poet, too, can be of service. " I am ambitious of doing the world some good," he wrote: " if I should be spared, that may be the work of maturer years." Much earlier he had declared, " I would jump down Ætna for any great Public good." Again he speaks of placing his " ultimate in the glory of dying for a great human purpose." And in the well-known letter to Taylor in which he confesses his need for knowledge and wisdom, he expresses his conviction most forcefully of all: " I find there is no worthy pursuit but the idea of doing some good to the world. Some do it with their society — some with their wit — some with their benevolence — . . . there is but one way for me. The road lies through application, study and thought. I will pursue it." " There is but one way for me, that is to prepare myself to write great poetry," he might have said. After all, that was the end of his study. For in spite of his mention of a wish to write on the "Liberal side of the question," when he was expressing a desire to be of some service to the world, after all he must have had in mind in these many iterations of his great longing to do some good, principally the doing of his best through poetry. In the pain of sickness and hopeless love during his latter days, he confided to Fanny Brawne his longing to write a poem to be a consolation for people in such a situation as his own. Yes, that would be it — a poem that by a fuller revelation of the meaning of life would assuage the doubts and fears of struggling souls, and lift the spirit to a higher plane. It would be a poem accomplishing its purpose by "bringing to utterance the Divine Nature, the deepest interests of humanity, and the most comprehensive truths of the mind."

But such a poem would have no moral tacked on to tell its tale, nor would its aim be to unravel any religious or moral problems. Such poetry needs no label to proclaim its messages. "Here are the Poems," wrote Keats to his brother and sister-in-law — "they will explain themselves — as all poems should do without any comment." Keats was a philosophic poet, as was Shelley, but equally with Shelley, he hated palpable didacticism.[7] We have seen how at times Keats almost idealized Wordsworth, but there were sides of the older poet that he thoroughly disliked, and one of these was his penchant for preaching and moralizing. This feeling led him at one time to denounce Wordsworth roundly. He is writing to Reynolds in February, 1818. The vigor of his sentiments may be taken as a measure of the intensity of his conviction:

It may be said that we ought to read our contemporaries, that Wordsworth &c. should have their due from us. But, for the sake of a few fine imaginative or domestic passages, are we to be bullied into a certain Philosophy engendered in the whims of an Egotist? Every

7 "Didactic poetry is my abhorrence; nothing can be equally well expressed in prose that is not tedious and supererogatory in verse." Preface to *Prometheus Unbound.*

man has his speculations, but every man does not brood and peacock over them till he makes a false coinage and deceives himself. Many a man can travel to the very bourne of Heaven, and yet want confidence to put down his half-seeing. Sancho will invent a Journey heavenward as well as anybody. We hate poetry that has a palpable design upon us, and, if we do not agree, seems to put its hands into its breeches pockets. Poetry should be great and unobtrusive, a thing which enters into one's soul, and does not startle it or amaze it with itself, but with its subject. How beautiful are the retired flowers! How would they lose their beauty were they to throng into the highway, crying out, "Admire me, I am a violet; dote upon me, I am a primrose!" Modern poets differ from the Elizabethans in this; each of the moderns, like an Elector of Hanover governs his petty state, and knows how many straws are swept daily from the Causeways in all his dominions, and has a continual itching that all the Housewives should have their coppers well scoured. The ancients were Emperors of vast Provinces, they had only heard of the remote ones and scarcely cared to visit them. I will cut all this — I will have no more of Wordsworth or Hunt in particular. Why should we be of the tribe of Manasseh when we can wander with Esau? Why should we kick against the pricks when we can walk on Roses? Why should we be owls, when we can be eagles? Why be teazed with "nice-eyed wagtails" when we have in sight the Cherub Contemplation? Why with Wordsworth's "Matthew with a bough of wilding in his hand" when we can have Jacques "under an oak" &c.? The secret of the Bough of Wilding will run through your head faster than I can write it. Old Matthew spoke to him some years ago on something, and because he happens in an Evening Walk to imagine the figure of the old Man, he must stamp it down in black and white, and it is henceforth sacred. I don't mean to deny Wordsworth's grandeur and Hunt's merit, but I mean to say we need not be teazed with grandeur and merit when we can have them uncontaminated and unobtrusive. Let us have the old Poets and Robin Hood.

One is glad to believe with Keats's contemporaries that this letter owed the evidence of rancor in it to a temporary fit of anger growing out of Wordsworth's careless characterization of *The Hymn to Pan* in *Endymion* as "a pretty piece of Paganism.[8]" It is certain, however, that the attitude towards the didactic expressed here is the result of permanent convic-

[8] See Houghton's comment in Forman. Vol. IV, p. 72. (Note.)

tion. The whole being of Keats rebelled at the idea of prostituting art, with its supreme function of interpreting and transmitting universal life truth, by any attempt to make it the vehicle of particular doctrine. Great art should be unobtrusive; it should be of the soul, speaking directly to the soul, of the hidden mysteries and patterns of life; it should never be the means of social, political, or religious propaganda.

CHAPTER X

WHAT IS POETRY?—CONCLUSION

A STUDY of what Keats has to say about art challenges one to attempt a formulation of his definition of poetry. The task is no easy one, for, in order to discover Keats's answer to the question, What is poetry? it becomes necessary not only to examine the young poet's direct utterance on the subject, but to take into account his whole aesthetic theory. Occasionally, one finds a near approach to a definition, but it is never complete and is intelligible only when linked with other passages of like import. It is convenient to begin with one of Keats's own attempts to explain what he thought great verse should be.

" In Poetry, I have a few axioms," wrote the young poet to his friend and publisher, John Taylor, in February, 1818, " and you will see how far I am from their centre.

1st. I think poetry should surprise by a fine excess, and not by singularity; it should strike the reader as a wording of his own highest thoughts, and appear almost a remembrance.

2nd. Its touches of beauty should never be half-way, thereby making the reader breathless instead of content. The rise, the progress, the setting of Imagery, should, like the sun, come natural to him, shine over him and set soberly, although in magnificence, leaving him in the luxury of twilight. But it is easier to think what poetry should be, than to write it. And this leads me to

Another axiom — That if poetry comes not as naturally as the leaves to a tree, it had better not come at all. — However it may be with me, I cannot help looking into new countries with ' O for a muse of Fire to ascend! ' "

Keats is emphasizing here one phase of poetry only, its effect upon the reader; but in his exposition of this, he touches upon the fundamentals that must lie behind that effect. " Poetry should surprise by a fine excess, and not by singularity." By surprise, Keats means to create a feeling of strangeness. This is not to result from singularity or the bizarre, such as the drapery from an Oriental setting or other distant scene; but rather, this effect is to consist in the largeness and fullness of imagery and feeling that is aroused in the pleasant recognition of one's own sincerest thoughts, which " appear almost a remembrance." This last seems to echo Wordsworth's " emotion recollected in tranquillity," and the whole idea recalls a remark of Walter Pater's: " A certain strangeness, something of the blossoming of the aloe, is indeed an element in all true works of art: that they shall excite or surprise us is indispensable. But that they shall give pleasure and exert a charm over us is indispensable, too; and this strangeness must be sweet also — a lovely strangeness." [1] This lovely excess, beauty never halfway, but luxuriant and luxurious, we find in most of Keats's poetry. It is found in its completest charm in some of the chastened descriptive scenes in *Hyperion:* it is at its fullest, freest splendor in the blending of beauty of sight and sound and inner sense into a symphony of loveliness in the *Eve of St. Agnes.*

Such fine excess and strangeness Keats found in much of Shakespeare. It is associated in his mind with a freedom and a fullness of imagination that must carry the poet into a region of his own creation, into a state of disentanglement from the particular facts and accidents of life and history. There are places where even the master poet fails in this, as Keats points out. But at his best, Shakespeare is the ideal artist, and Keats's critical remarks on Shakespeare are always instructive as to his own ideas of poetry. Speaking of the history plays and the three parts of *Henry VI*, he says:

They are written with infinite vigour, but their regularity tied the hand of Shakespeare. Particular facts kept him in the high road, and would not suffer him to turn down leafy and winding lanes, and to

[1] *The Poetry of Michelangelo,* in *The Renaissance.*

break wildly and at once into the breathing fields. The poetry is for the most part ironed and manacled with a chain of facts, and cannot get free; it cannot escape from the prison house of history, nor often move without our being disturbed with the clanking of its fetters. The poetry of Shakespeare is generally free as is the wind — a perfect thing of the elements, winged and sweetly colored. Poetry must be free! [2] It is of the air, not of the earth; and the higher it soars the nearer it gets to its home. The poetry of "Romeo and Juliet," of "Hamlet," of "Macbeth," is the poetry of Shakespeare's soul — full of love and divine romance. It knows no stop in its delight, but "goeth where it listeth " — remaining, however, in all men's hearts a perpetual and golden dream. The poetry of "Lear," "Othello," "Cymbeline," &c., is the poetry of human passions and affections, made almost ethereal by the power of the poet. Again, the poetry of "Richard," "John," and the Henries is the blending the imaginative with the historical: it is poetry! but oftentimes poetry wandering on the London Road.[3]

This last quotation is rich in the essence of Keats's ideas on the nature of poetry. In *Henry VI,* particular facts kept Shakespeare " on the high road, and would not suffer him to turn down leafy and winding lanes, and to break wildly and at once into the breathing fields." Here is the criterion of luxuriance, of " fine excess " boldly applied to Shakespeare. " Do not the lovers of poetry like to have a little region to wander in, where they may pick and choose, and in which the images are so numerous that many are forgotten and found new in a second reading; which may be food for a week's stroll in the summer? " Keats asks elsewhere, in argument against Hunt's query, " Why endeavor after a long poem? " Keats's own imagination was tropical and demanded a poetical garden of rich abundance.

" Poetry must be free! It is of the air, not of the earth; and the higher it soars the nearer it gets to its home." — The

---

[2] " In short," says Hazlitt, " it is to take the language of imagination from off the ground, and enable it to spread its wings where it may indulge its own impulses, without being stopped or fretted, that poetry was invented." *On Poetry in General.*

[3] *The Champion.* Sunday, Dec. 28, 1817. Forman. Vol. III, pp. 234–235.

poetry of *Richard, John,* and " the Henries " is to Keats inferior, for, even though there is here a blending of the imagination with the historical, yet the earthly touch is too obtrusive, and it is at best " poetry wandering on the London Road," poetry not triumphantly free, but chained by particular facts.

Does Keats mean then that in the best poetry there must be a complete escape from the earth and the earthy? Part of the foregoing might suggest such a conclusion. But read down a few lines: " The poetry of ' Romeo and Juliet,' of ' Hamlet,' of ' Macbeth,' is the poetry of Shakespeare's soul — full of love and divine romance." And further: " The poetry of ' Lear,' ' Othello,' ' Cymbeline,' etc., is the poetry of human passions and affections made almost ethereal by the power of the poet."

In this direct discussion of the characteristics of true poetry Keats reveals the fundamental antithesis that marks so much of his aesthetic thought — the conflict between a desire for escape and a sense for reality. The difficulty is apparent.

It is obvious that poetry of " the human passions and affections " cannot be a literature of escape, no matter how much etherealized. It must have its genesis in a knowledge of mankind and in imaginative insight into the human soul. Such poetry cannot be entirely free, cannot soar indefinitely near heaven, its home, for always it must be bound to the unchanging actualities of existence. To be sure, it can get away from the certain particular facts of history, but it cannot escape life.

As we have seen, a great deal of Keats's aesthetic theory is concerned with an attempt to reconcile these conflicting claims; and with his progress toward reconciliation came greater clarity as to the nature and function of poetry. Consequently, before we can go on with our definition, it will be necessary to review briefly the ground already covered in this book.

It would seem that in the beginning of his poetic career, Keats had only a general notion of what it was all about. At first, he appears to have felt that it was only necessary to give the imagination free rein, especially when under the influence of nature, and poetic vision would result. The content was not clearly defined. In the early poems of 1815 and 1816 knights, ladies, and nymphs, chivalry and love would seem to be the principal objects, though there is a suggestion of more substantial, more serious earthy subjects, as parts of the three epistles of the period would indicate. In *Sleep and Poetry,* however, there is a clear-cut enunciation of the theory that all other delights in poetry must yield to the nobler life of humanity, where the poet shall " find the agonies and strife of human hearts." Then came the rich aesthetic experiences of 1817, the period of the first acquaintance with the Elgin Marbles, the period of a new reading and understanding of Shakespeare, of a serious study of Wordsworth at Oxford, and of the " burning of thought " on poetry on the Isle of Wight. Keats was at this time seeking for that " centrality," which Professor Irving Babbitt declares the Romantic poets lack. " The truly Romantic universe," says Mr. Babbitt, in his *Rousseau and Romanticism,* " has no centre."

The young Keats early began to realize that his poetic universe was indeed without a centre; but he was not content to let it remain so. He set himself to analyze; he sought to define the nature of the world in which he was living and the poetic relationships of the various elements of that world to each other. *Endymion* was the first result of this thinking.

Keats's universe, as revealed in *Endymion,* does have " centrality," only imperfectly expressed perhaps, yet truly existent to him who will study the poem carefully in the light of the whole of the poet's writings. The universe of *Endymion* is made up, first, of the surface and seeming of life, visible, sensuous things; second, of humanity, with all its passions and sorrows; third, of an invisible existence behind all this, of which, it develops as Keats's meaning unfolds itself, the first two are but a part: for in the end, the heavenly dream-maiden of Books I and II symbolizing the realm of the sensuous, the

Indian Maiden representing humanity, and Cynthia, embodying the ideal world, prove to be identical.[4] Later, Keats was to define these conceptions more clearly. In his comments on the mighty abstract Idea of Beauty[5] and in the letter on the Imagination to George and Georgiana Keats, of December, 1818,[6] he clearly suggests that the nature of this invisible world can be known only through a knowledge of the reality about us, which the creative imagination makes its starting point in the building of an abstract universe of which all that can be seen and known is but a small part. The world of sense is incomplete and can furnish but a clue to the vast invisible reality. Further, in his discussion of the world as a " vale of Soul-making " Keats suggests his belief in an animating principle pervading the universe, a God, who throws off soul sparks. These, through contact with a world of pain and troubles admirably fitted for the work of soul-making, develop into identities and individualities, which at death must pass back into the all-soul. Here, too, we find expressed a conviction as to a higher law, which neither man nor nature can evade. There is no escape from the world as it is: when " fish philosophize the ice away in winter-time," then can man change the order of things in this world, no sooner.

The conception of an unchanging order is also manifest in *Hyperion*. The action of this poem represents the operation of an " eternal law," so inflexible that even a " primeval god " cannot change so much as the beginning of a day. According to this law, too, the evolutionary processes of the world go on, and to the eternal decree

That first in beauty should be first in might,

all creatures, both gods and men, must bow. Keats uses in

[4] See Chap. III, p. 62. Also Bridges, Introduction to the G. Thorn Drury edition of Keats, p. XXIII. Mr. Bridges' particular interpretation is somewhat different, but he was the first critic to point out the identity of the three objects of Endymion's love.

[5] See Chap. VIII, p. 156.   [6] Chapter VII, p. 110.

different places, different names for the transcendent power. In *Endymion,* the unseen presence is the Moon, or Cynthia, or again *essence* or *immortal love;* in the passage on the vale of Soul-making it is God; in *Hyperion,* Cœlus apostrophizes the sun-god as

> . . . brightest of my children dear, earth-born
> And sky-engendered, Son of Mysteries
> All unrevealed even to the powers
> Which met at thy creating. (Book I, ll. 309–312.)

But *essence, love, God,* or *powers,* whatever the appellation, the eternal invisible was to Keats a very real, dynamic existence, which he felt the true poet must know and understand.

Of this universe man is the centre. In *Endymion,* Cynthia, the symbol of the ideal world, the embodiment of all-that-is-worth-knowing, is indeed the apparent object of the poet's desire, but she is reached and apprehended only through a close communion with, and understanding of, humanity and through sympathy with human misery and sorrow: in fact, she is finally discovered to be identical, as an ideal of poetic endeavor, with man. The chief business of the poet then comes to be to know the human heart to its depths and to interpret it to the world. This idea is expressed with infinitely greater clarity in the Mansion of Life letter of 1818, where a comparative "anxiety for humanity," an ability "to think with the human heart," the capacity to sharpen one's "vision into the heart and nature of man," and the power to convince "one's nerves that the world is full of misery, and heartbreak, pain, sickness, and oppression," are made the tests by which a great poet must be measured. It is repeated with unmistakable emphasis in the revised *Hyperion,* of 1819, when Moneta abjures the aspiring poet that the one way to enter the high sanctuary of true poetry is to know and feel the suffering and misery of the world until there can be no rest.

It would appear from this then, that Keats was at least one romanticist who had sought and found "centrality." He had discovered it not in the high serenity of Greek poetry and sculpture, which found its repose in a self-contained world where disturbing speculations as to the universe beyond seldom obtruded — the complexities of modern thought would not permit that, neither would his own nature, and he could not if he would escape the conviction of a supersensuous world; he had not permitted himself to be lured into seeking it, as did weaker spirits of his age, in vague and indefinable longings for the secrets of a mysterious, invisible existence: but, rather, he sought for this centrality in wisdom through knowledge and " continual burning of thought " upon the facts of poetry and existence as he found them. And, with remarkable clarity of judgment, he came to the conviction that all that can be known or imagined as to a world beyond visible reality must be deduced from that reality itself, that there is no more valid basis for an understanding of the infinite than a thorough knowledge of the finite, especially a knowledge of the human heart itself, which, to know in its fullness and profundity, is to know the burden of the mystery; and, since it is in the darkest, most tragic and miserable hours of life that the soul of man approaches nearest to infinite and god-like capacities, then that poet understands most of all-that-is-desirable-to-know who has probed to the depths the most profound misery, pain, and heartbreak of the great suffering heart of humanity.

Thus Keats linked his metaphysical speculations with his aesthetic. It led him direct to the world in which we live for his materials for poetry, which should be great in proportion as in it the most significant of human experiences and the sharpest of men's passions should be portrayed.

But it must be remembered that Keats came to this conclusion, marking as it did a decisive antithesis to his original idea of imaginative detachment, only after a severe struggle. It was a conflict that really continued on down to the end, for it involved the two opposing fundamentals in his aesthetic thought, which as we have seen were probably never quite reconciled.

Keats began with an apotheosis of the imagination. Revery merging into the ecstatic trance seemed to him the condition for poetic vision. Thus, he felt, the old Greek poetry must have come into being. However, as we have seen, he early perceived that great poetry must have a serious aspect and must reflect the deeper experiences of life. But at first, he only vaguely perceived the means to this end. We may suppose that by the time *Sleep and Poetry* was finished, though Keats understood to some extent that the great poet must know the human heart before he can ascend to the heights of poetic power, he knew no other process whereby this knowledge might be obtained than that of emotional revery and direct divination. It would seem that even in *Endymion,* while there is evidence of a higher plane of thought on the part of Keats, and the poem as a whole emphasizes the need of knowing mankind, the principal means to this knowledge is the feelings. And at the end of 1817, about the time *Endymion* was completed, Keats is exclaiming, in exaltation of the imagination and in rebellion against philosophy, " O for a life of sensations rather than of thoughts! "

But shortly after this came the advance in his thinking of the spring of 1818, which drove him to accept knowledge and philosophy as necessary elements to insight. He was now to seek knowledge through every possible avenue, through books, reasoning, experiences, travel, contacts with men. But even in the early months of 1818, during which the balance had swung so strongly toward knowledge, there are evidences of rebellion and reaction. For practically at the same time that he is declaring that he means to follow Solomon's directions and " Get learning — get understanding " — for he has found that he " can have no enjoyment in the world but continual drinking of knowledge," he is also writing such lines as those entitled *What the Thrush Said,* which reflect an entirely different attitude:

> O fret not after knowledge. I have none
> And yet my song comes native with the warmth.

> O fret not after knowledge! I have none,
> And yet the evening listens.

It is a case of conflict between head and heart, between an impulse to complete abandonment to imaginative flights and a will to a rigid discipline of the poetic faculties through knowledge and philosophy. Another bit of verse written at this time admirably demonstrates the nature of this schism, and at the same time points the way to reconciliation. " Hence Burgundy, Claret, and Port," exclaims the poet,

> Too earthly ye are for my sport;
> .   .   .   .
> My bowl is the sky,
> And.I drink at my eye,
> Till I feel in the brain
> A Delphian pain —

But this draught of ethereal nectar is not an unreproved and free pleasure, as the apostrophe to Apollo that follows shows:

> God of the Meridian,
>   And of the East and West,
> To thee my soul is flown,
>   And my body is earthward press'd. —
> It is an awful mission,
>   A terrible division;
>   .   .   .   .
>   . . . God of Song,
> Thou bearest me along
>   Through sights I scarce can bear:
> O let me, let me share
>   With the hot lyre and thee,
> The staid Philosophy.
>   (*A Draught of Sunshine.* January 31, 1818.)

The conflict is severe, but not a hopeless one. Not only here but in other poems and letters of the period a near reconciliation is suggested. In the sonnet on *King Lear,* where he exclaims,

> Let me not wander in a barren dream,
> But, when I am consumed in the Fire,
> Give me new Phoenix wings to fly at my desire,

and in the passage from his May letter to Reynolds in which
he explains the difference between sensations with and without knowledge — without knowledge, " we are falling continually ten thousand fathoms deep and being blown up again,
without wings, and with all the horror of a bare-shouldered
creature," with knowledge, " our shoulders are full fledged
and we go through the same air and space without fear " —
Keats shows that the imagination is to be still triumphant.
Only now it is to be educated; it will no longer be irresponsible, unguided soaring, but will be the activity of a seeing
power in which the whole intellectual and emotional life of
the poet is concentrated.

If the young poet could only have fully accepted this
reasoned judgment now, along with his conclusion that the
real world and the human heart must be the object of poetic
insight, he could have been at peace with himself. But
there were too many subsidiary problems left unsolved. The
operations of the imagination seemed too complex to be so
easily disposed of. Its capacity for complete insight, for
identification, for projection of itself into the lowest or highest entities; its creative powers, with its ability to construct
ideal worlds of its own; in general, its inherent tendency to
unrestrained, unshackled flight — all this insistently demanded
recognition. And then there were times when the whole
hideous business of the world bore so upon Keats's senses as
to make escape seem imperative, as in the *Epistle to Reynolds,*
when, after describing the heartless cruelty of it all,

> . . . where every maw
> The greater on the less feeds evermore,

he exclaims that he is still " sick of it," for

> Still do I that most fierce destruction see,
> The Shark at savage prey, — the Hawk at pounce
> The gentle Robin like a pard or ounce,
> Ravening a worm.

" Away ye horrid moods! " he cries, in feverish revulsion,

and one understands how deeply these vivid images of the grim bloody struggle for existence in the animal world have cut into his soul, and one realizes, too, how difficult it was for an individual of such temper to live at peace with a world where this cruelty seems such a commonplace as to be accepted by the generality as a mere matter of course, scarce worth a comment.

Yet Keats seemed to feel that in order for a poet to interpret life adequately he must find a way to this peace; in other words, the poet must be in harmony with the world in which he is living. Taine, commenting on this same problem, once declared that " there are indeed but two modes of agreeing with the world: mediocrity of mind and superiority of intelligence — the one for the public and the fools, the other for artists and philosophers: the one consists in seeing nothing, the other in seeing all." Keats likewise perceived but two possible paths to agreement: one was to shut out the actualities of existence and flee away to a dream-world; the other was to face the realities of life squarely, to see and understand all. Strongly as his young instincts urged him to follow the first course, Keats's deeper judgment taught him that his artistic salvation lay in his turning to the latter as the necessary basis for the creation of great poetry. But often the task he had set for himself seemed too much for him. He frequently found himself unable to accept the facts of life and be content; instead of the harmony he desired, he sometimes found himself sick at heart and distracted, sadly loathing the whole machinery of a brutal creation. It was in such moods that he wrote *The Epistle to Reynolds* and those letters to Bailey in which he rebelled at the thought that delicate women must have cancers and must suffer in childbirth.[7] At such times he evidently found the whole problem of reconciling himself to reality so difficult that he was tempted to renounce a poetic creed that demanded an understanding of, and harmony with, the world as it is, and

7 See Chapter V.

flee for refuge to the sunny warmth of an entirely ideal universe.

The consequence is we find Keats continuing to express an impulse to aesthetic escape and a revulsion against " philosophy," as in *To a Nightingale* and in *Lamia*. But in spite of these emphatic reactions, he was ever advancing toward a more complete reconciliation between the demands for detachment and the claims of actuality. He came to see that no matter how alluring the poetic dream-world, no matter how necessary it may be for the poet to enter it in his periods of artistic creation, this dream-world itself must be built upon the foundations of the real. He was working toward a conception of a calm, contemplative, penetrative activity for the poet, who might view the world with all knowledge, but, in the wisdom of perfect understanding, escape its fevers and fret, beholding even in cruel or apparently purposeless acts something fine as material for poetry.

This in no way bars the imagination; it merely provides a means for the sensitive soul of the poet to bear with a harsh world while he accumulates the knowledge and philosophy necessary to great production. At any rate, in the end, all must be dissolved and re-created in the fires of the poetic imagination, which in its highest form is the one supreme poetic faculty, the most authentic guide to truth and beauty, the vital constructive shaping spirit in poetry and all art.

In the *Fall of Hyperion*, we have Keats's most mature thought on this subject. Whether it would have been his final word had he lived, one cannot tell. But it would seem that a poet could advance little beyond an acceptance of the doctrines expressed in the scene between Moneta and the poet in the first book. The poetic aspirant is seeking to ascend the steps to the high altar in the temple of poetry; he is in a trance, Keats's orthodox condition for entering the poetic dream-world. But just as in *Endymion* when the poet would rush madly and blindly after the vision of the ideal, he is taught that he must be lessoned in the great school of Nature and humanity before he can reach his goal, the poet is here sternly told how useless it is to seek the poetic heights until to him " the miseries of the world are misery, and will not let him rest." Keats is saying that a simple, natural response to the beauties of the world cannot alone make a poet; moreover, that mere aimless projections of the imagination are not the stuff out of which poetry is made: that is mere dreaming, and a poet who tries to build on such a basis is a weak visionary. The secret of real poetic achievement lies in an intuitive insight enriched by knowledge and thought, actual contact with mankind, genuine experience with the pains and sorrows of humanity. Only with such a disciplined imagination can the veil to the " Mystery " be pierced. Like Ralph Touchett's ghost, the " Mystery " can be seen only by those who have " suffered first, have suffered greatly, have gained some miserable knowledge." [8] In that way the eyes are opened to the meaning of human life in its relationship and unity with the ineffable spiritual forces of the universe.

That which the intellectualized and experienced imagination apprehends is truth; and to see a thing in its truth is also to see it in its beauty, that is, in its deepest, most universal aspects, yet emotionalized, living, vital. There came a time to Keats when Grecian beauty meant not pleasant revery upon the old mythology, but rather warm recreation of Grecian life, a lively perception of something of the meaning of it all, a vivid sense of the onward rush of the universe, as in his brain there grew a dizzy pain in the intuition of " Grecian grandeur " mingled with the " rude wasting of old time." The quest for Beauty then became to Keats a search for the heart of spiritual verity as it was to be found in the most significant experiences of existence. The business of the poet, as a discoverer and interpreter of this Beauty, consequently comes to be to catch the quiet, mysterious overtones of life and to body them forth in objective forms of truth and power. Beauty is found

[8] Henry James. *Portrait of a Lady*, p. 40.

in a work of art, Keats felt, only when there is within it
something to grip the imagination, something that rouses the
mind to a full and free speculative activity and reveals to it,
in a pleasant glow of apprehension, inexpressible thoughts
and visions of almost ethereal meanings.

This, of course, is beauty in its deeper and more philosophic
sense. Keats was also a lover of beauty in its purely sensuous
aspects. The lovely in sound, color, and form struck upon his
senses with a pleasure akin to exquisite pain. It was the
melody and smoothness of Spenser's poetry that early won his
applause; his own line, " Spenserian vowels that elope with
ease," gives a clue as to a quality the young poet much admired in his early master. The harmony of Milton's verse,
moving on like music throughout, " like a grand accompaniment to the Base of Heaven," excites his warm praise. He
was so sensitive to the beauties of nature that " the humming
of a bee, the sight of a flower, the glitter of the sun, seemed
to make his nature tremble," his eyes flash, his cheeks glow,
and his mouth quiver; the motion of " the inland sea " — the
passage of a violent wind over a field of oats or barley — was
sufficient to transport him entirely out of himself; in his last
illness, he fondly recalls the loveliness of the English spring:
" . . . how astonishingly does the chance of leaving the world
impress a sense of its natural beauties upon us! Like poor
Falstaff, though I do not ' babble,' I think of green fields; I
muse with the greatest affection on every flower I have known
from my infancy.— " Keats did indeed love external beauty.
But, after all, for the true poet, this loveliness is only secondary, and at its best is chiefly significant as an aid in expressing
the inner soul of things, the final aesthetic beauty and truth
of being. Thus the *Ode on a Grecian Urn* has for its main
theme, not the sensuous beauty of the marbles described, but
the imaginative pictures that the artistic representations
arouse. The urn is lovely to look at, but the poet gives this
loveliness mere passing notice. His real interest is in more
vital elements. What Keats does in this great ode is to give

us his most authentic interpretation of a typical aesthetic experience. Here we have that which may be considered the young poet's ideal of what should be the effect of a great work of art? And what should be that effect? In a word, beauty — the vision of truth flashed upon the inner eye in moments of aesthetic concentration. In its mere sensuous aspects the urn represents specific acts of particular individuals: the " mad pursuit " of maidens, the " struggle to escape," the warm music of love, the " wild ecstasy " of excited wooing by impassioned youths; quieter love-making, with the gentle melodist in the sweetness of spring bowers " for ever piping songs for ever new " to his young mistress in the shade; religious ceremonies that have emptied a peaceful little town of all its folk, to follow the " mysterious priest " and the fated heifer, richly garlanded, and " lowing at the skies," toward the sacrificial pyre. But the quality that raises all this to the plane of high art is the power of the artist to suggest through these figures the motives, the emotions, the ideals, the life-principles that lie behind the representations — what these people felt, believed, experienced, what might be their significance in the vast procession of human creation.

What the observer gets is much what the original artist got, an intuitive perception of the indefinable mysteries of existence, an insight into the deepest human experiences and into the essential unity of the soul of man with the universal all-spirit of the universe. It is not mathematical nor scientific truth that is revealed; it is, instead, that shadowy inexpressible sense of truth, which not the intellect and understanding alone grasp, but rather one's whole illumined, emotionalized being. " Thou, silent form, dost tease us out of thought as doth eternity," exclaims Keats. That is, there are no ends, no boundaries to this sort of knowledge, any more than to eternity. Its limits are set only by the restrictions to man's free speculative activity. Yet it is none the less real and genuine for all that; rather it is perhaps the nearest approach to the ultimate all-truth yet open to finite minds.

So with poetry. Melody, charm, loveliness, all great verse should possess, but only as subsidiary adjuncts to its deeper function, the conveying of truth.

Taking this as an ideal for his own work, the poetry that Keats would create should accurately convey the vision of the poet; its every phrase should ring with the "voice of true feeling," and the least word and sound should be chosen to that end. At the same time there should be a fullness of imagery in it: "its touches of beauty should never be half-way"; it "should surprise by a fine excess." But in it all there should be such a universal human quality that "it should strike the reader as his own highest thoughts and appear almost a remembrance." That Keats placed this universal quality above other consicerations, especially above mere ornamentation and strangeness of effect, is to be seen from the testimony of John Hamilton Reynolds, long most intimate with the young poet on these matters, in an article in which he explained and defended his friend's theories.[9] Reynolds writes of Keats:

His feelings are full, earnest, and original, as those of the olden writers were and are; they are made for all time, not for the drawing-room and the moment. Mr. Keats always speaks of, and describes nature, with an awe and a humility, but with a deep and almost breathless affection. — He knows that Nature is better and older than he is, and he does not put himself on an equality with her. You do not see him, when you see her. . . . Poetry is a thing of generalities — a wanderer amid persons and things — not a pauser over one thing, or with one person. The mind of Mr. Keats, like the minds of our older poets, goes round the universe in its speculations and its dreams. It does not set itself a task. The manners of the world, the fictions and the wonders of other worlds, are its subjects. . . . The true poet confines his imagination to no one thing — his soul is an invisible ode

[9] In the fall of 1818, John Hamilton Reynolds replied to the savage attacks of the *Quarterly Review* and *Blackwoods Magazine* by an article in the *Alfred, West of England Journal* (October 6, 1818). Reynolds and Keats had been on such terms of intimacy that we may be sure that when Reynolds essays here to describe Keats's ideas of poetry, he may be almost thought of as Keats himself speaking. The passage is quoted by Forman. Vol. IV, p. 178.

to the passions — He does not make a home for his mind in one land — its productions are an universal story, not an eastern tale. . . .

Here are many of the best things Keats himself might have written of poetry, not only of its universality, but of its permanence, its sincerity, its depth. The soul of the poet, " is an invisible ode to the passions." Keats himself had declared, in the spring of 1817, describing his ideal in poetry, " The poetry of ' Romeo and Juliet,' of ' Hamlet,' of ' Macbeth,' is the poetry of Shakespeare's soul, full of love and divine romance. . . . The poetry of ' Lear,' ' Othello,' ' Cymbeline,' etc., is the poetry of human passions and affections, made almost ethereal by the power of the poet." This early description of great poetry gives the clue, after all, to such a definition as Keats might have written in December, 1819. He could at most only have expanded upon it and particularized; for, as he went on, he saw ever more clearly that great poetry has its genesis in the universal human heart and that the soul of the poet must vibrate in unison with that heart, that he must possess the wisdom and sympathy to understand it to its depths, and then must have the power of imagination and the creative ability almost to etherealize his vision and crystallize it into forms of beauty and of truth. With Keats the object of poetry is to interpret, to give the sense of the inner mystery of life and nature that we may know them in their essential qualities, not as science presents them but, as Matthew Arnold suggests, by awakening in us " a wonderfully full, new, and intimate sense of them and our relations with them."

It is apparent that up to the end, Keats felt that he had never realized his ideal. He planned to write plays, and looked forward to a time when he might have wealth of experience and depth enough to nerve himself to his chief attempt in drama. He looked upon the drama as the highest form in poetry and longed to revolutionize it, even as Kean had acting. But from the first, the poet understood that before he could be fitted for that he must subject himself to a long period of apprenticeship. He told himself that he must first pass through the "regions of Flora and old Pan" before he could enter the higher realms of human passions. The writing of *Endymion* was but an exercise that could scarce take him "a dozen paces towards the temple." "The high Idea I have of poetical fame," he tells his brother George, "makes me think I see it towering too high above me." And to Hunt, he declares, "I have asked myself so often why I should be a poet more than any other man, seeing how great a thing it is — how great things are to be gained by it, what a thing to be in the mouth of Fame — that at last the idea has grown so monstrously beyond my seeming power of attainment, that the other day I nearly consented with myself to drop into a Phaeton. Yet 'tis a disgrace to fail, even in a huge attempt; and at this moment I drive the thought from me."

But, luckily, Keats did not drop "into a Phaeton," and he did not fail. For though he did not reach his lofty goal, he certainly approached it. In *Hyperion*, the stage is set for a poem in which the deepest miseries are revealed, and in the mental suffering of deposed Saturn sunk "deep in the shady sadness of a vale," where Gods speak "much as they might have been supposed to speak," Keats is indeed getting into the borderlands of his poetic ideal. But he felt failure. A year after the first *Hyperion*, he was expressing his wish to "diffuse the colouring of St. Agnes Eve, throughout a poem in which character and sentiment would be the figures to such drapery." And even such poems would merely be stepping stones: "Two or three such Poems, if God should spare me, written in the course of the next six years would be a famous gradus ad Parnassum altissimum. I mean they would nerve me up to the writing of a few fine Plays — my greatest ambition."

There is in all of Keats's writings, no passage more illuminating than this: it flashes light into remote recesses of his aesthetic thought otherwise all dark; it is at once a revelation of what he thought great poetry ought to be and a commentary on how such poetry can be created. The *Eve of St. Agnes*, beautiful, melodious, luxuriant in sensuous imagery, was looked upon by Keats merely as a finger exercise in preparation for the high tasks to follow. Exquisite as were its sensuous beauties, they were at best fitted to serve but as external " drapery " for the great poems of " character and sentiment," he hoped to create in the full perfection of his powers. In these works — dramas, representing men in action, in conflict, under stress of powerful emotions — mere prettiness and triviality, all superficiality and mawkishness would be banished. And in their place, drawn from a heart made wise by life's most vital and thrilling experiences, would appear depth of insight, truth and sincerity of line and sentiment, intensity of human passion.

As I have indicated, it would seem that in Keats's own works his theory of what great poetry should be is best exemplified in his *Hyperion* and *The Fall of Hyperion*. The scene is better portrayed in the *Hyperion;* the poetic theory is the more apparent in the Revision. But for the present purpose it is unnecessary to differentiate between the two poems. The Hyperion story is a story of evolutionary progress; that I have already pointed out. But it is also something more: it is tragedy, supreme, irrevocable tragedy — the tragedy of downfall and defeat. Ancient Saturn and all his compeers of the old order, save Hyperion, have been ruthlessly deposed and cast out of heaven. Beings of pristine splendor, born to power and uncontested rule, now suddenly overthrown and supplanted by a younger more brilliant dynasty before whose might resistance is folly, their sufferings are tremendous. Hyperion alone, in proud, regal magnificence, still reigns on; but knowing full well that he, too, is to fall, he lives in weak, ungodlike dread. All this is laid bare to the soul-penetrating vision of the poet, who, having qualified himself through knowledge of the misery of the world, has been permitted to ascend the high altar of poetic truth, where, under the guidance of his monitress Moneta, in one supreme imaginative leap, he finds himself in a position from which he may see and understand everything.

From this point, setting himself " Upon an eagle's watch "

that he may see, " and seeing ne'er forget," the poet con-
templates the tragedy of the fallen gods. And as he looks
there grows " a power " within him

> of enormous ken
> To see as a god sees, and take the depth
> Of things as nimbly as the outward eye
> Can size and shape pervade.
>
> (*The Fall of Hyperion.* Canto I, ll. 278–281.)

This is the point of Shakespearian " Negative Capability," of
" innate universality," that Keats has before shown himself
to crave as his poetic goal.

Imbued with god-like power to penetrate into the depths of
human experience, the poet now records what he perceives.
His characters in the allegory are gods, but these gods talk
like men, and their sufferings and passions are those of men
under stress of like fundamental intense and tragic life-experi-
ences. Here are rage, hate, revenge, hope, fear, despair; here
are misery, abasement, shame, humiliation; here, also, are kind-
ness, love, and sad sympathy: all represented with an insight
and poetic power that mark the *Hyperion* torsos, fragmentary
though they are, as on a par with some of the grandest poetry
in the English language. Surely, we have here one of those
" two or three such poems " of " character and sentiment "
that were to nerve the young poet " in the course of the next
six years " to his " chief attempt in the drama." How the
world must ever regret that those six years were not allotted
to this gifted young singer that he might have had opportunity
to bring his dreams to something near fruition!

The high idea Keats had of real poetic achievement led him
to look upon years of toil in preparation and experimentation
as a logical and natural requirement in the " gradus ad Parnassum altissimum." He had humbly set himself to the long
task of ascending the heights; he had advanced far up the
steep slopes and had written poetry of immortal accents; but
he was not permitted to attain to his lofty ideal — death came
too soon.

BIBLIOGRAPHY

THE WORKS OF KEATS

ERNEST DE SELINCOURT: *The Poems of John Keats.* Dodd Mead and Company. 1905.

H. BUXTON FORMAN: *The Complete Works of John Keats.* Five Volumes. Gowans and Gray, London. 1901.

H. BUXTON FORMAN: *The Poetical Works and Other Writings of John Keats* (Library Edition). Four Volumes. Reeves & Turner, London. 1883.

H. BUXTON FORMAN: *The Poetical Works of John Keats.* Three Volumes. J. B. Lippincott Company. 1891.

H. BUXTON FORMAN: *The Letters of John Keats.* Reeves and Turner, London. 1895.

RICHARD MONCKTON MILNES: (Lord Houghton): *Life, Letters, and Literary Remains of John Keats.* In Two Volumes. Moxon, London. 1848.

LORD HOUGHTON: (Richard Monckton Milnes): *Life and Letters of John Keats* (The New Universal Library Edition). George Routledge and Sons, London.

SIDNEY COLVIN: *The Poems of John Keats in Chronological Order.* Two Volumes. The Florence Press, Chatto and Windus, London, 1917.

SIDNEY COLVIN: *Letters of John Keats.* Macmillan & Company, London. 1891.

WILLIAM T. ARNOLD: *The Poetical Works of John Keats.* Kegan Paul, Trench, & Company, London. 1884.

W. T. YOUNG: *Poems of Keats, Endymion. The Volume of 1820 and Other Poems.* Cambridge University Press. 1917.

M. R. HILLS: *Keats Odes, Lyrics and Sonnets.* Oxford University Press. London. 1916.

ARTHUR C. DOWNER: *John Keats: The Odes.* Oxford, The Clarendon Press, 1897.

ERNEST DE SELINCOURT: *Hyperion, A Facsimile of Keats's Autograph Manuscript.* Oxford, The Clarendon Press. 1905.

JOHANNES HOOPS: *John Keats' Hyperion.* Heidelberg. Carl Winter's Universitätsbuchhandlung. 1898.

CRITICISM

SIDNEY COLVIN: *John Keats: His Life and Poetry, His Friends, Critics, and After-Fame*. Charles Scribner's Sons. 1917.

F. M. OWEN: *John Keats, A Study*. C. Kegan Paul & Company, London. 1880.

D. G. Rossetti: *Life of John Keats*. Walter Scott, London. 1887.

SIDNEY COLVIN: *Keats* (In English Men of Letters Series). Macmillan and Company, London. 1887.

AMY LOWELL: *John Keats*. Houghton Mifflin Company, 1925.

S. J. MARY SUDDARD: *Keats, Shelley, and Shakespeare; Studies and Essays in English Literature*. Cambridge, University Press. 1912.

ALBERT ELMER HANCOCK: *John Keats*. Houghton Mifflin Co. 1908.

LUCIEN WOLFF: *John Keats, Sa Vie et Son Oeuvre*. Hachette & *Cie*, Paris. 1910.

H. I'A. FAUSSET: *Keats, A Study in Development*. Secker, London. 1922.

MATTHEW ARNOLD: *Essays in Criticism*. Second Series. Macmillan and Co. 1888.

J. M. ROBERTSON: *New Essays Toward A Critical Method*. John Lane. 1897.

J. W. MACKAIL: *Lectures on Poetry*. Longmans, Green and Co. 1911.

A. C. BRADLEY: *Oxford Lectures On Poetry*. Macmillan & Co. 1909.

ROBERT BRIDGES: Introduction to the G. Thorn Drury Edition of Keats's Poems. George Routledge and Sons, London. 1894.

HALL CAINE: *Cobwebs of Criticism*. E. Stock, London. 1883.

HENRY C. NOTCUTT: *An Interpretation of Endymion*. South African Electric Printing Co., Capetown, South Africa. 1919.

H. A. BEERS: *History of English Romanticism in the 19th Century*. Henry Holt and Company. 1899.

LEIGH HUNT: *Lord Byron and Some of His Contemporaries*, Two Volumes. Colburn, London. 1828.

WILLIAM J. COURTHOPE: *The Liberal Movement in English Literature*. J. Murray, London. 1885.

ALGERNON SWINBURNE: *Miscellanies*. Chatto and Windus, London. 1886.

WILLIAM GRAHAM: *Last Links with Byron, Shelley, and Keats*. Leonard Smithers & Company, London. 1898.

COWDEN CLARKE: *Recollections of Keats*. Atlantic. VII: 90.

JOSEPH SEVERN: *Vicissitudes of Keats's Fame*. Atlantic. XI: 401.

The John Keats Memorial Volume. The Bodley Head. 1921. MR. DE SELINCOURT: *The Warton Lecture on Keats;* LACELLES

ABERCROMBIE: *The Second Version of Hyperion;* JOHN BAILEY: *The Poet of Stillness;* A. C. BRADLEY: *Keats and " Philosophy ";* A. CLUTTON–BROCK: *Keats and Shelley. A Contrast;* SIDNEY COLVIN: *A Morning's Work in Hampstead Garden;* W. P. KER: *Note on Hyperion;* AMY LOWELL: *The Lost Letter of Keats;* ARTHUR LYNCH: *John Keats;* J. W. MACKAIL: *A Note on the Composition of Endymion;* GEORGE SAINTSBURY: *A Reminiscence of Endymion;* G. BERNARD SHAW: *Keats;* ARTHUR SYMONS: *A Note on John Keats;* FREDERICK BOAS: *On First Looking Into Chapman's Homer;* ARTHUR LYNCH: *John Keats.*

JAMES RUSSELL LOWELL: *Literary Essays.* Houghton Mifflin and Company. 1890.

STOPFORD A. BROOKE: *Studies in Poetry.* G. P. Putnam's Sons. 1907.

WILLIAM J. DAWSON: *The Makers of Modern Poetry.* Whittaker. 1902.

J. MIDDLETON MURRY: *The Problem of Keats.* The Athenaeum. July 25, 1919.

R. D. HAVENS: *Influence of Milton on English Poets.* Harvard University Press. 1922.

DAVID MASSON: *Wordsworth, Shelley, Keats, and Other Essays.* Macmillan and Company. 1874.

J. J. JUSSERAND: *Histoire Abrégée de la Littérature Anglaise.* C. Delegrave, Paris. 1896.

GEORGE SAINTSBURY: *A History of Nineteenth Century Literature.* Macmillan and Company. 1896.

C. H. HERFORD: *John Keats,* in *The Cambridge History of English Literature.* G. P. Putnam's Sons.

S. GEEST: *Der Sensualismus bei John Keats.* C. A. Wagner. Freiburg Im. Breisgau. 1908.

PAUL STARICK: *Die Belesenheit von John Keats und die Grundzüge Seiner Literarischen Kritik.* Mayer & Müller, Berlin. 1910.

W. A. REED: *Keats and Spenser.* Ph. D. Dissertation, Heidelberg. 1897.

JOHANNES HOOPS: *Keats' Briefe in Ihrem Wert für die Charakteristiks des Dichters.* Anglia, XXIV, p. 133. 1901.

TOM TAYLOR: *Life of Benjamin Robert Haydon.* Three Volumes. Longmans, London. 1853.

GEORG BRANDES: *Main Currents in Nineteenth Century Literature.* W. Heinemann, London. 1901–'05.

C. H. HERFORD: *Shakespeare's Treatment of Love and Marriage and Other Essays.* T. F. Unwin, London. 1921.

OTHER WORKS CONSULTED

EDWIN BJÖRKMAN: *Is There Anything New Under the Sun?* M. Kennerley. 1911.

IRVING BABBITT: *Rousseau and Romanticism.* Houghton Mifflin Company. 1919.

A. C. BRADLEY: *English Poetry and German Philosophy in the Age of Wordsworth.* Manchester, The University Press. 1909.

A. S. COOK: *The Art of Poetry.* Ginn and Company. 1892.

J. C. SHAIRP: *Aspects of Poetry.* Houghton Mifflin Co. 1882.

CHARLES AND MARY COWDEN CLARK: *Recollections of Writers.* Sampson Low. 1878.

WILLIAM SHARP: *The Life and Letters of Joseph Severn.* Sampson Low. 1892.

BENJAMIN ROBERT HAYDON: *Correspondence and Table Talk. With a Memoir by His Son, Frederic Wordsworth Haydon.* Two Volumes. Chatto and Windus, London. 1876.

LEIGH HUNT: *Imagination and Fancy.* Second Edition. Smith, Elder, and Company, London. 1845.

LEIGH HUNT: Autobiography. Two Volumes. Harper & Brothers. 1860.

LEIGH HUNT: *Essays,* Edited by Arthur Symons. The Walter Scott Publishing Co., London, 1887.

GEORGE SAINTSBURY: *A History of English Prosody.* Macmillan and Company. 1910.

THOMAS CARLYLE: *Sartor Resartus.* Edited by J. A. S. Barrett. A. C. Black, London. 1897.

SAMUEL COLERIDGE: *Biographia Literaria.* Everyman's Edition. E. P. Dutton and Company.

HEGEL: *The Philosophy of Fine Art.* Four Volumes. Translated, With Notes, by F. P. B. Osmaston, B.A. G. Bell and Sons, London. 1920.

GEORGE SANTAYANA: *Three Philosophical Poets.* Cambridge, Harvard University. 1910.

GEORGE SANTAYANA: *Interpretations of Poetry and Religion.* C. Scribner's Sons. 1900.

GEORGE SANTAYANA: *The Life of Reason.* C. Scribner's Sons. 1905–06.

PLATO: *Works.* Jowett translation. Bigelow, Brown & Co., New York.

HAZLITT: *Spirit of the Age and Lectures on English Poets.* 1818. Everyman's Library. E. P. Dutton and Company.

KANT: *Kritik of Judgment.* Translated by J. H. Bernard. Macmillan and Company. 1892.

B. BOSANQUET: *The Value and Destiny of the Individual.* Macmillan and Company, London. 1913.

BENEDETTO CROCE: *Aesthetic as Science of Expression and General Linguistic.* Translated by Douglas Ainslee. Macmillan and Company, London. 1909.

DEWITT HENRY PARKER: *Principles of Aesthetics.* Silver Burdett and Company. 1920.

E. F. CARRITT: *The Theory of Beauty.* The Macmillan Company. 1914.